CLIMBING BEYOND

First published in Great Britain
2017 by Aurum Press an Imprint of The Quarto Group
The Old Brewery
6 Blundell Street
London N7 9BH

A catalogue record for this book is available from the British Library.

ISBN 978 1 78131 598 9
Ebook ISBN 978 1 78131 714 3

10 9 8 7 6 5 4 3 2 1
2021 2020 2019 2018 2017

Designed by The Urban Ant Ltd.
Printed in China

CLIMBING BEYOND
The World's Greatest Rock-Climbing Adventures

James Pearson & Caroline Ciavaldini

Contents

1 Devil's Bay

2 Yosemite

3 White Rim

4 The Deep South

6 Salto Angel

5 Patagonia

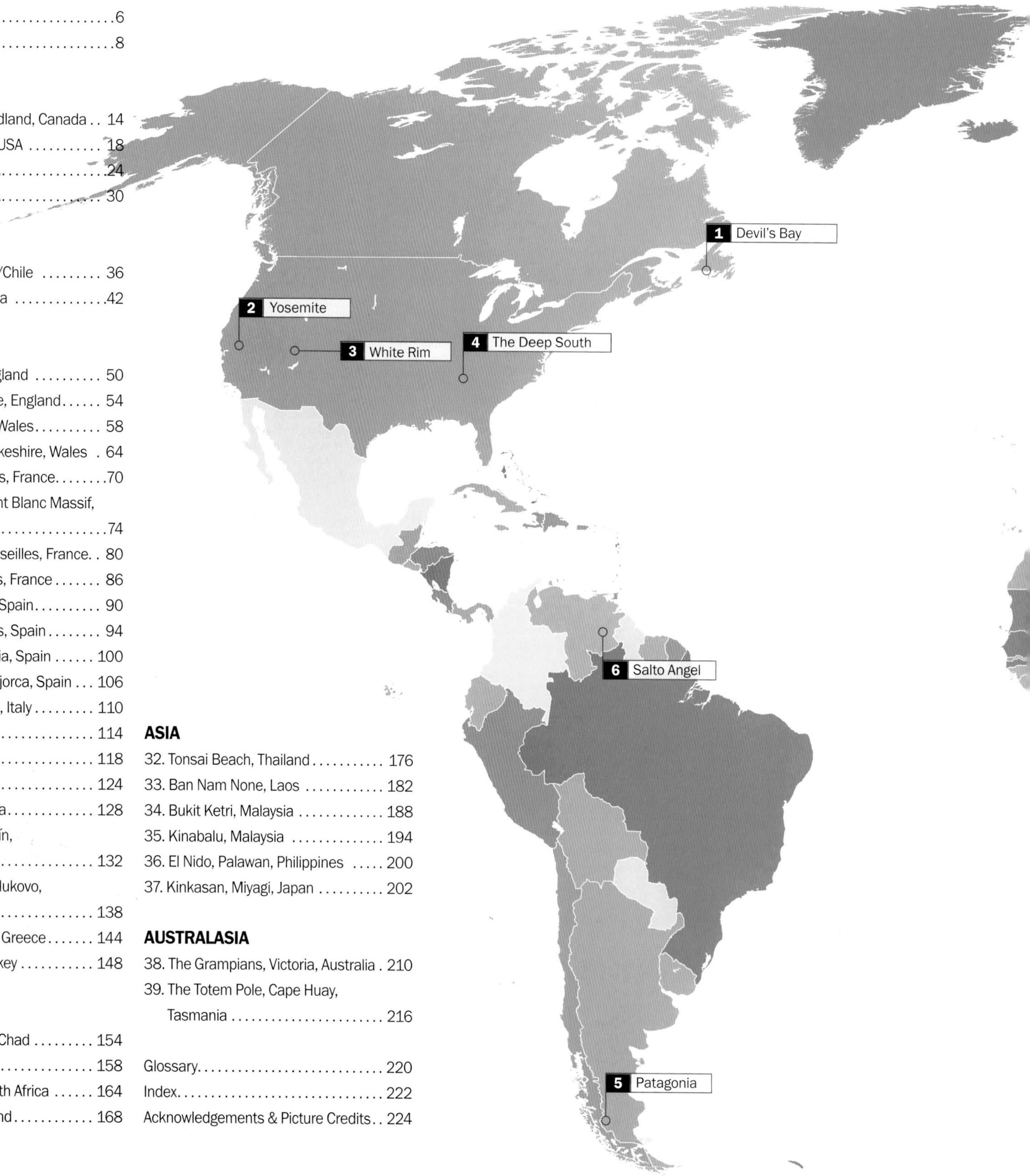

9 The Slate

7 The Peak District

10 St Govan's

8 Nesscliffe

24 Elbe Valley

22 Ticino

14 Fontainebleau

21 Rätikon

12 Grand Capucin

23 Zillertal

11 Céüse

25 Prohodna Cave

16 Roca Verde

19 Qualido

13 Les Calanques

17 Montserrat

26 Metéora

15 La Pedriza

20 Aria

18 Cova del Diablo

27 Kaynaklar

37 Kinkasan

29 Tafraout

33 Ban Nam None

28 Ennedi Desert

32 Tonsai Beach

36 El Nido

34 Bukit Ketri

35 Kinabalu

31 Cilaos

30 The Cederberg

38 The Grampians

39 The Totem Pole

Foreword
Tim Kemple

How lucky are we to have such an awesome excuse to travel the planet through climbing? Whether you are an alpinist, sport climber or boulderer, we share an incredible common bond that gives us a reason to explore some of the most epic landscapes on Earth and opens the door to friendships that last a lifetime.

I grew up climbing in cold and wet New England, USA – far from the giant granite walls of Yosemite that I dreamed of scaling as a kid – so I know exactly how it feels to make trips to far-away lands in the name of climbing. We used to do the drive to the Valley in a non-stop, 42-hour push, taking turns sleeping in the back of my old Volvo station wagon. They were epic road trips, but they were always full of short-lived glimpses of passing lands and friends that we never had enough time to enjoy along the way. We'd return home with stories of tall granite walls, but nothing about the journey in between. Growing up reading climbing magazines, ALL you thought about was the destination – but it turns out that the journey is where the fun happens.

That's when I learned my most valuable lesson as a traveller: that it's one thing to see a new country at 65 mph from the comfort of an air-conditioned car, and quite another to immerse yourself in the nuanced culture, place and presence of a new land. Maybe it's that your life is literally hanging by a thin thread, but climbing demands appreciation for the holistic approach of discovery. After all, attention to detail is

paramount for success. As climbers we dream of these epic places and become obsessed with the small irregularities in the stone that make every climb unique. And details take time and patience to learn. Luckily the journey doesn't stop after the sun goes down, so when it's time to come in from the cold of the mountains, our common passion has a way of opening doors to places, homes and basecamp tents, even if you can't speak the local language. That's the real gift of climbing – an excuse to travel the globe and meet the new best friends that you never knew you had.

It wasn't long before that 42-hour drive to Yosemite became a week-long adventure with stops to see friends in Kentucky, Colorado and Utah. And soon I was travelling overseas, chasing new cliffs and seeking new friendships. It was on one of these 'expeditions' that I first met James Pearson in a rural village in China. We were both about as far from home as we could physically be, but our common thirst for adventure helped create a friendship that has seen us connecting on yearly pilgrimages for nearly a decade.

I've learned many things from James, and later his wife Caroline, over the years, but none more important than the fact that no matter how new the place, or foreign the language, you have to commit to pushing yourself out of your comfort zone. I still remember vividly a rest day in China, when the rest of the team just wanted to type away on their computers. James rented a scooter and went on a solo mission to explore new climbs and caves. He returned hours later, way after dark, with tales of getting stuck in the mud, getting lost and nearly getting into several accidents. You could tell from the smile on his face, though, that his 'rest day' was one of the most memorable of the trip. The moral of the story? You shouldn't travel halfway across the world just to sit in a hotel room, or your tent. James is always the first to remind me of this.

So as you flip through these pages, I hope that you'll be inspired by James and Caroline's unrivalled enthusiasm – but also remember that it's not just about the climbs, but also about the journey and great people you experience along the way. See you out there!

LEFT: Hazel Findlay trying to stay motivated above a foggy and wet basecamp in Devil's Bay, Newfoundland.

Introduction

Do we travel to climb, or climb to travel?

That's a question we have been asking ourselves recently – where exactly do our priorities lie?

In the early days, everything was so simple. Climbing was new and exciting – something that, once tasted, had to be consumed, and often to excess. Caroline and I (James) come from two very different worlds, and yet surprisingly our climbing motivation followed strikingly similar paths. Notice I say 'climbing motivation' and not just climbing. Our actual climbing couldn't have been more different, Caroline being focused on indoor competitions, a style of climbing where one's safety is never in question, and me drawn by the daring and danger of British trad climbing.

Caroline grew up on the tiny French island of La Réunion, a dot on the map off the east coast of Madagascar. Climbing was one of many sports she enjoyed at school as a child, and for one reason or another it's the one that stuck. On Réunion Island, sport means competition. At the age of 12, Caroline began structured climbing, training with a club, and before long her evenings and weekends were devoted to it. She quickly rose through the junior ranks, the poor quality of the local climbing walls offset by pure motivation, winning the French Youth Climbing Championship aged 15.

In the UK, things were a little different. The public perception of climbing was one of extremes – of brave daredevils, hanging on for dear life by their fingertips. By comparison with France, where climbing was offered at most public schools, it was once very hard for a youngster to begin climbing in the UK unless they were lucky enough to have family or friends already in that world. As it was, and despite a longing to do so from as far back as I can remember – and a habit of climbing anything and everything I could – it wasn't until I made some new friends at secondary school, who by chance turned out to be climbers, that I could try 'real' rock climbing for the first time. The gritstone of the Peak District became my teenage playground, one where I would spend any and every free minute of my day. The quality and quantity of hard routes to test my skills and nerve seemed limitless. Why would I ever need to go anywhere else?

RIGHT: Caroline Ciavaldini leading
the third pitch on Zembrocal,
Réunion Island.

As a reward for winning the youth championship, the French National Climbing Federation invited Caroline to watch a 'real' world cup in France. The realization quickly sank in that if she wanted to cut it in that world of climbing superstars, Réunion Island would have to be left behind. She left Réunion aged 16 to move to Montpelier, home at the time of the French Youth Training Centre, and devoted herself to that world. Over the next ten years she would enjoy a career as one of France's top competition and sport climbers, visiting exotic places all around the globe, yet ironically rarely seeing more than the inside of the hotel and the climbing gym. At that time competitions were all, and everything was focused on performance. A climbing gym in one city was just like that in any other, providing new routes to test her skills and develop her climbing repertoire, and the possibility of competing against the other top climbers in the world.

Whilst the gritstone outcrops of the Peak District were still my main target, my progression as a climber had begun to slow, and the realization that climbing on different rock types might help me to build and develop new skills had started to set in. Travelling locally at first – and, as finances allowed it, further afield – I always left home with a specific objective in mind, hoping that what I learned on my travels would allow me to climb ever-harder challenges when I returned.

After meeting in 2010 and beginning a relationship that would eventually lead to marriage, Caroline and I slowly began to open our eyes. While trad climbing and competitions were important, perhaps there was more out there than just difficult routes, and we began to plan our initial trips together with the simple objective of seeing the world. Southeast Asia provided the backdrop for our first adventure, and in addition to discovering several fantastic new climbing areas, we also met many wonderful people, and for a fleeting moment in time were let into their world. We saw first-hand what it was like to raise a young family in the jungle of Laos, and spent a day dodging checkpoints with petrol smugglers on the north Malaysian border.

On returning home, we saw just as much, if not more, interest in those stories than in our regular climbing feats. This surprised us at first, yet on reflection it made perfect sense. Climbing performance alone will always remain somewhat abstract, but human experiences and emotions are things to which we can all relate. We began to travel more, often making trips back to back, and spending ever less time at home. We'd record our trips with video and photos, sometimes for publication in international climbing magazines and sometimes just for us. As time went by, our drive and motivation shifted. Performance in the moment became less of a focus, replaced by the desire to fill our memory banks with stories to tell our grandchildren in some distant future time. Eventually we started Once Upon A Climb (onceuponaclimb.co.uk), our platform for creating and sharing our stories, and something that we hope to see grow over the coming years.

Climbing Beyond is a collection of some of our favourite climbing destinations from around the world. Obviously, being our own interpretation, this list is very subjective and there are many fantastic destinations that didn't make the cut. Caroline and I are not your average climbers and, as I've done my best to explain here, we prefer to walk the road less travelled. This is reflected in this book, and the selected areas and routes often have an adventurous feel to them.

Within each chapter you will find stunning photos, thanks to the many talented photographers we have had the chance to work with over the years. Thank you to you all – this book would not have been possible without you. You will also find historical and logistical information, as well as a map or a topo of the area or route. This book should not be mistaken for a climbing guide, however, for while the information within will give you a general idea of a climb or an area, any aspiring adventurer will need to do their own, more in-depth research, should they ever decided to turn dreams into reality.

Nor should this book be mistaken for our personal climbing diary. Whilst we have fantastic personal memories from many of the included destinations, we chose to keep our descriptions neutral in the hope of allowing the reader to visit without any preconceived ideas. After all, the reason we love to travel is to discover another view of this world – if we told you exactly what to look for, you wouldn't have to open your eyes so wide.

Climbing is a wonderful gift. Have fun out there!

James Pearson and Caroline Ciavaldini

Understanding the grade variations

The 'grades' that climbers use to quantify their routes are a subject that could warrant a book in their own right. The table below aims to make a comparison between the various grading scales of different countries and climbing styles, but one should always remember to take grades with a pinch of salt as they are, after all, only a guide. For each chapter of this book, we have chosen to to list the grades in the format normally used in that area. Whilst this may be a little confusing at first, this table will help you to understand, as well as develop and expand your knowledge of the different scales in use around the world.

British Trad Grade (for bold routes) ladder, shown as diamonds: Mod (Moderate), Diff (Difficult), VDiff (Very Difficult), HVD (Hard Very Difficult), Sev (Severe) 3c, HS (Hard Severe) 4a/4b BOLD, VS (Very Severe) 4b/5a BOLD/SAFE, HVS (Hard V Severe) 4c/5a/5b BOLD/SAFE, E1 5a/5b/5c BOLD/SAFE, E2 5a/5b/6a BOLD/SAFE, E3 5b/6a BOLD/SAFE, E4 5c/6a/6b BOLD/SAFE, E5 6a/6b/6c BOLD/SAFE, E6 6b/6c BOLD/SAFE, E7 6c/7a BOLD/SAFE, E8 6c/7a BOLD/SAFE, E9 7a/7b BOLD/SAFE, E10 7a/7b BOLD/SAFE, E11 7b/7b SAFE.

Sport Grade	UIAA	USA	Norway	Australia	South Africa
1	I	5.1		4	6
2	II	5.2		6	8
2+	III	5.3	3	8	9
3-	III+	5.4	4	10	10
3	IV	5.5			11
3+	IV+	5.6	4+	12	12
4	V-	5.7	5-	14	13
4+	V	5.8	5	15	14/15
5	V+	5.9	5+	16	16
5+	VI-	5.10a	6-	17	17
6a	VI	5.10b	6	18	18
6a+	VI+	5.10c		19	19
6b	VII-	5.10d	6+	20	20
6b+	VII	5.11a	7-	21	21
6c	VII+	5.11b		22	22
6c+	VIII-	5.11c	7	23	23
7a	VIII	5.11d	7+	24	24
7a+		5.12a		25	25
7b	VIII+	5.12b	8-	26	26
7b+	IX-	5.12c		27	27
7c	IX	5.12d	8	28	28
7c+	IX+	5.13a	8+	29	29
8a	X-	5.13b		30	30
8a+	X	5.13c	9-	31	31
8b		5.13d		32	32
8b+	X+	5.14a	9	33	33
8c	XI-	5.14b	9+	34	34
8c+	XI	5.14c		35	35
9a		5.14d		36	36
9a+	XI+	5.15a		37	37
9b	XII-	5.15b		38	38
9b+	XII	5.15c		39	39

BOULDERING GRADES

V Grade	Font Bouldering Grade	British Tech Grade
VB	3	4a
V0-	3+	4b
V0	4	4c
V0+	4+	5a
V1	5	5b
V2	5+	5c
V3	6a / 6a+	6a
V4	6b / 6b+	
V5	6c / 6c+	6b
V6	7a	
V7	7a+	
V8	7b / 7b+	
V9	7c	
V10	8a	
V11	8a+	
V12	8a+	
V13	8b	
V14	8b+	
V15	8c	

North America

Devil's Bay Newfoundland, Canada
Grade variation: 5.9 to 5.12d

Until very recently, the hard granite of Newfoundland's Devil's Bay was the playground of a few 'in-the-know' New Englanders. Around two hours by boat from the nearest town, which is itself four hours from the nearest road, Devil's Bay feels like the end of the world. The combination of violently changeable weather and unrelenting biting insects adds to the hellish nature of this aptly named place. So why would anyone want to spend their holidays climbing here? The answer is simple – because there are few places on this Earth where one can establish new routes on perfect rock rising majestically 400 metres directly out of the ocean.

The main cliff of Devil's Bay is known locally as 'Blow Me Down', a name that makes sense the moment you first set eyes on it. Starting off directly out of the water with gentle slabs, Blow Me Down rises ever steeper from the sea like some gigantic, frozen wave. Free-climbing routes are kept to the more vertical extremes of the cliff, with the imposing overhangs in the middle of the wall making way for only one or two optimistic aid lines, hinting at possibilities the future could bring.

When all is well in Devil's Bay, it is a rather wonderful place to be. The campsite is situated a stone's throw from the cliff face, with flat, rocky platforms protruding from a gently sloping grassy hill, all sitting alongside a glacier-fed stream. Views look out over a wide ocean fjord, with rocky cliffs and waterfalls as far as the eye can see. The sun comes out, temperatures soar, and you find yourself asking why so few people know about this place.

BELOW: Laundry time, with a perfect
view of the picturesque basecamp.

However, should Mother Nature have other ideas, one can find oneself shrouded in thick, drenching mist for days on end, with even the gigantic mass of Blow Me Down hiding out of sight. The nights bring winds so strong that they destroy all but the most hardy of tents, and the tranquil stream flowing through the centre of camp becomes a raging torrent that threatens to carry you away to the ocean below.

The most valuable skill a visiting climber can possess is patience, for one never knows when the terrible weather will break. Fortunately, with the cliff being so close to the campsite – and having so much free time to prepare one's equipment – when the opportunity for climbing does finally arrive, you can be on the rock with very little time wasted. Due to the nature of its general form, routes on Blow Me Down tend to become more difficult as the climber ascends. This makes for a very enjoyable outing, allowing oneself several pitches to warm up before the real difficulties are met. The rock is bullet hard and very featured, offering both well-protected cracks and scary, run-out face climbs. Protection comes mostly in the form of natural trad gear, but there is the odd bolt and piton on some of the harder sections and blank-face pitches.

A recent trip to Devil's Bay was led by Mark Synnott, who was tipped off about its potential by some of Blow Me Down's original New England pioneers. Mark and his team of fellow The North Face athletes had hoped to open up several new lines through the steeper sections of the cliff, but Mother Nature had other ideas.

'We were hit by one of the worst storms I can remember and spent almost two weeks hunkered down in our tents,' recalls Mark. 'Each day we hoped to get out on the rock, each day we were left disappointed, and pretty soon even the beer and junk food we'd lugged up to the camp failed to lift our spirits. When confinement became too much, we would hike off into the unknown wilderness, often in torrential rain, in an effort to simply appreciate the incredible rugged beauty of the place.'

He continues, 'We did manage to get out for a few hours here and there, repeating some of the classic existing lines end even putting up our own new route. These climbs were of amazing quality and really hint at what else Blow Me Down has to offer.'

Devil's Bay is a magical and mystical place that, despite being part of the western world, feels as isolated as the most unknown parts of our globe. It can feel like hell on Earth, but if you get lucky and play the weather and elements at their own game, it offers the opportunity for amazing new routes as well as some of the hardest big-wall trad climbing around.

BELOW, LEFT: Unfortunately the basecamp was also a wind tunnel!

BELOW: The basecamp dome was our salvation during the days of endless rain.

BOTTOM: The vital equipment packed on pallets, ready to be loaded.

RIGHT: The mist rolling down the hillside was a constant companion on this trip.

Fact File Devil's Bay

TYPE OF CLIMB: Adventure, multi-pitch, trad

TYPE OF ROCK: Granite

GRADE VARIATION: 5.9 to 5.12d

CLIMB LENGTH: 400m

BEST TIME TO CLIMB: May to September

OTHER NOTABLE CLIMBS: Leviathan, 5.12a

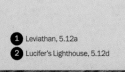

Devil's Bay

1 Leviathan, 5.12a

2 Lucifer's Lighthouse, 5.12d

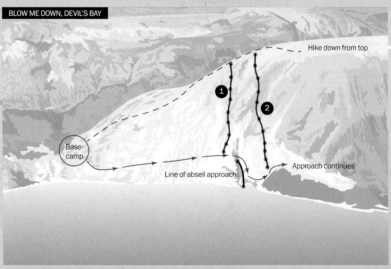

BLOW ME DOWN, DEVIL'S BAY

Hike down from top

1

2

Base-camp

Line of abseil approach

Approach continues

Yosemite California, USA
Grade variation: Limitless

There are few climbing areas in the world with a reputation as big as Yosemite Valley in California, a place whose standing in the climbing world is matched only by the size of its cliffs. The American climbing grading scale was invented here – the YDS, or Yosemite Decimal System – as Yosemite Valley was one of the first places in America to see climbing evolve into its own separate sport. People have been climbing here since the late 1800s, and its climbs and cliffs have been documented in thousands of books and guides. Its longevity as an iconic destination speaks to its uniqueness: Yosemite is like no other place on Earth.

Yosemite's individuality comes not only from its majestic walls, but from the way that people from all backgrounds and walks of life can come together to enjoy the magic of this valley. The giant rock walls here are open to interpretation, from multi-day aid ascents to sub-one-hour solos.

BELOW: The classic 'Tunnel View',
the first view of Yosemite Valley when
you arrive.

Yosemite's walls have seen it all, and continue to provide for the dreams and desires of a rapidly evolving sport.

Royal Arches (5.9, 16 pitches), now considered to be one of the valley's easiest long routes, was once upon a time just a dream for the climbers of their era. It was first attempted and eventually climbed in the autumn of 1936 by Morgan Harris, Ken Adam and Kenneth Davis, using pioneering new rope techniques such as 'the pendulum', which would later become commonplace on many of Yosemite's climbs. Royal Arches was a milestone achievement in Yosemite's climbing history, hinting at the possibilities that these giant walls might one day yield.

Nowadays, a skilled climber can solo Royal Arches in a few hours, and the speed record sits at a mind-blowing 52 minutes from car to car. Yet one does not need an exceptional level of skill to enjoy this route – quite the contrary. Royal Arches can be enjoyed by just about anyone, and it's far more usual to see a roped party of two or three pass a stunning day climbing its 16 pitches to the summit.

There are, however, a few challenges in Yosemite that are only possible for the very best – climbers so skilled and visionary in their approach and dedication that they leave us 'mere mortals' shaking our heads, mouths open, and wondering. Alex Honnold is one such climber, a man who, for the last seven years has been redefining what is possible. Honnold is undoubtedly the world's most famous living climber, and has been featured in major newspapers, TV shows and adverts. Yet despite his superstar standing, Alex remains true to his 'dirtbag' roots, living out of his converted campervan and travelling the world, simply climbing.

Alex began climbing at an indoor climbing gym in Sacramento, California, and by the age of 18 he was one of the best competition climbers in the country. After dropping out of college he borrowed the family minivan and embarked on a two-year-long road trip that would begin to define the rest of his life. Struggling to find regular climbing partners, he began to solo easy climbs, slowly increasing the difficulty and developing his skills until he was on a par with the greatest free-soloists to have come before him. In 2008, Alex took a step beyond anything that had been done before when he free-soloed the northwest face of Half Dome, one of the biggest cliffs in the valley at over 600 metres high. This achievement saw Alex's career explode, and this shy, unassuming kid from northern California became an American household name almost overnight.

Since that day, Alex has continued to develop his free-soloing skills and has accomplished many more unbelievable feats around the world, from Malaysia to Mexico. It is to Yosemite Valley that he keeps on coming back, however, either to push the standards of the future or to relive the amazing memories of the past. Yosemite is a playground for everyone, and we are lucky to have it.

HALF DOME, YOSEMITE

Thank God Ledge

The Zigzags

Big Sandy

The Chimneys

Robbins Traverse

Regular Northwest Face, 5.12a, 23 pitches

Fact File Yosemite

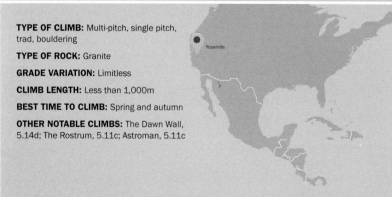

Yosemite

TYPE OF CLIMB: Multi-pitch, single pitch, trad, bouldering

TYPE OF ROCK: Granite

GRADE VARIATION: Limitless

CLIMB LENGTH: Less than 1,000m

BEST TIME TO CLIMB: Spring and autumn

OTHER NOTABLE CLIMBS: The Dawn Wall, 5.14d; The Rostrum, 5.11c; Astroman, 5.11c

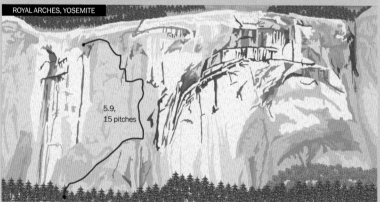

ROYAL ARCHES, YOSEMITE

5.9, 15 pitches

RIGHT: Alone on the wall: Alex Honnold's most famous solo of Half Dome.

White Rim
Canyonlands National Park, Utah, USA
Grade variation: 5.10 to 5.14+

The Monument Basin – or Canyonlands National Park – has to be one of the final unexplored frontiers of rock climbing in North America. In a country where cars, 4x4s and bicycles have touched almost every inch of land, there are precious few spots remaining where barely a footstep has been placed.

The 1,377 square kilometres of the Canyonlands National Park are found in the state of Utah, close to the tiny desert city of Moab. Accessible only via the infamous White Rim Road, this 114-kilometre dirt track is passable only by 4x4 high-clearance vehicles, mountain bikes and on foot. The area has been accessed for many years – first by uranium miners in the 1950s and later on by adventurous off-road tourists – but it still remains almost untouched by climbers, with miles and miles of unclimbed sandstone walls, towers and deep, dark caves just waiting to be discovered.

Most climbers who visit this out-of-the-way place do so for the obvious huge, standing towers that dot the edge of the White Rim. Standing Rock, Washer Woman and Block Top, to name just a few, draw in aspiring climbers from around the world. Yet tucked away underneath the White Rim itself, out of sight of almost everything except perhaps the local wildlife, is a whole different world that attracts a particularly masochistic breed – the off-width climber.

Over millennia water has washed down through the surface cracks of the White Rim rock and eroded the softer shale underneath, leaving thousands of caves just out of view. Access to these caves is extremely difficult, in many cases requiring special climbing equipment or a great deal of personal risk. The caves can seem almost cathedral-like in their sheer size and presence. When entering one for the first time, you have the odd feeling of being somewhere incredibly special but at the same time feeling slightly out of place. There are occasional signs of human passage as well as sparse, forgotten encampments of Native American hunters, but apart from that it is a place almost entirely untouched by man.

TOP LEFT: Tom Randall and Pete Whittaker trying to get a feel for the place in the Canyonlands Visitors' Center.

BOTTOM LEFT: Breakfast in the back of the truck.

OPPOSITE: The endless roof cracks under the White Rim.

NEXT PAGE: Tom Randall checking out a futuristic roof-crack project.

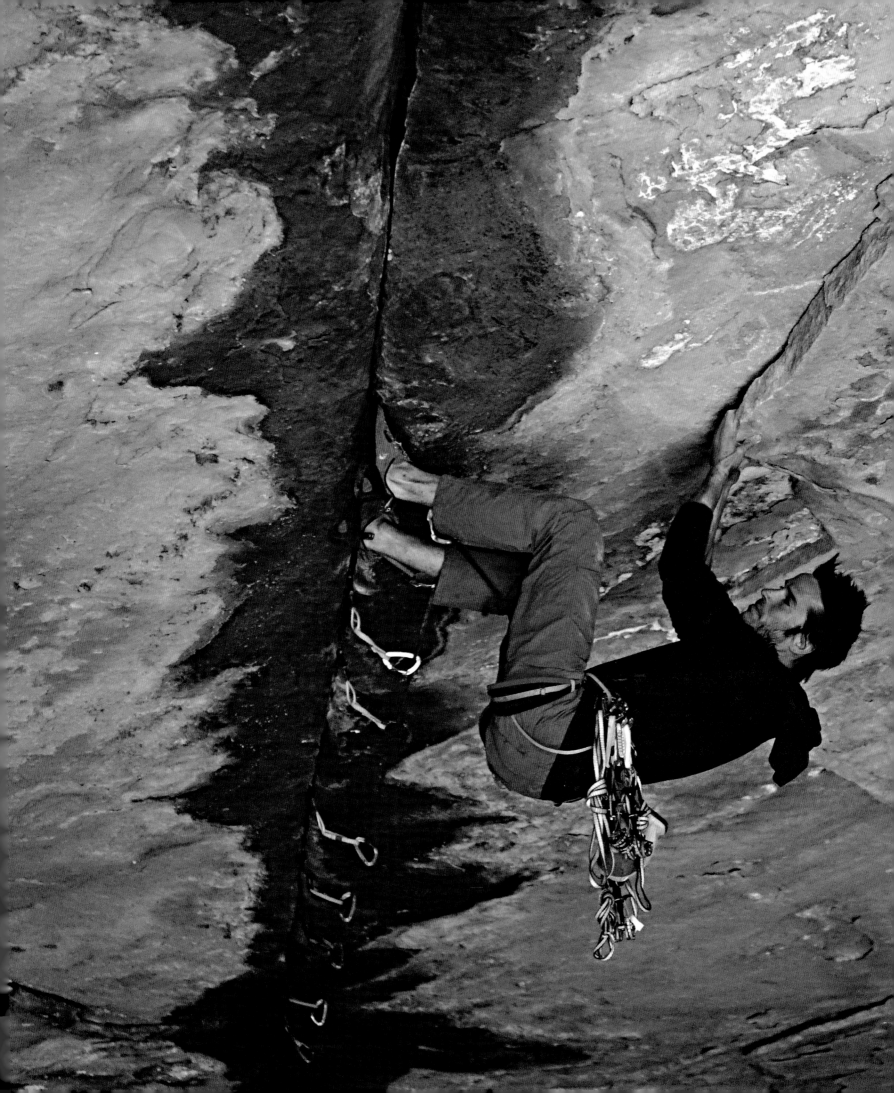

Fact File White Rim

TYPE OF CLIMB: Trad, roof cracks

TYPE OF ROCK: Sandstone/mudstone

GRADE VARIATION: 5.10 to 5.14+

CLIMB LENGTH: 20 to 50m

BEST TIME TO CLIMB: October to April

OTHER NOTABLE CLIMBS: Crown of Thorns, 5.14; Millennium Arch, 5.14

Canyonlands National Park

CENTURY CRACK, WHITE RIM

Abseil to canyon floor

5.14

Scramble into cave

'WE REALIZED THAT WITH only a short period in which to explore, we must have only touched the surface.' – Tom Randall

In 2011, off-width crack-climbing specialists Pete Whittaker and Tom Randall headed to the White Rim to attempt an unfinished climbing project known as the 'Century Crack'. Having heard various reports from several highly respected off-width climbers, the young Brits wanted to find out for themselves if this thing really was as long and as hard as everyone had said. After several weeks of visiting most of the classic crack-climbing areas in the US, Pete and Tom got stuck into Century Crack and, to the surprise of almost everyone in the States, made rapid, back-to-back ascents of what was supposed to be the hardest crack climb in the world.

For the last few years the pair have travelled the world, repeating and establishing many of the most difficult crack climbs on the planet and training in between trips in the tiny basement of Tom's terraced house in Sheffield. Each as obsessed as the other, their dream is to find the 'one true line', justifying countless hours of monotonous pain and torture. Finally, having come full circle, the pair returned to Canyonlands in early 2016, determined to take things to the next level.

'Our love affair with the White Rim did not end in 2011,' Tom explained. 'We realized that with only a short period in which to explore, we must have only touched the surface. There were still thousands of caves that had never been explored and possibly there could be more potential. We returned in 2016 in an attempt to map out the best caves and climbing projects and to try to locate a route that could be truly special. After one month of exploring almost the entire underside of the White Rim by 4x4 and on foot, we located what could be the longest and hardest roof crack in the world – The Crucifix Project.'

Inaccessible, dangerous and impossibly difficult it may be, but any trip to Canyonlands will always be well worth the effort.

ABOVE: Exploring the horizontal plane of Canyonlands.
OPPOSITE, TOP: Finding new routes requires a lot of searching.

OPPOSITE, BOTTOM LEFT: Pete Whittaker using binoculars to check out the other side of the rim.
OPPOSITE, BOTTOM RIGHT: With a lack of solid abseil anchors, the truck proved very useful.

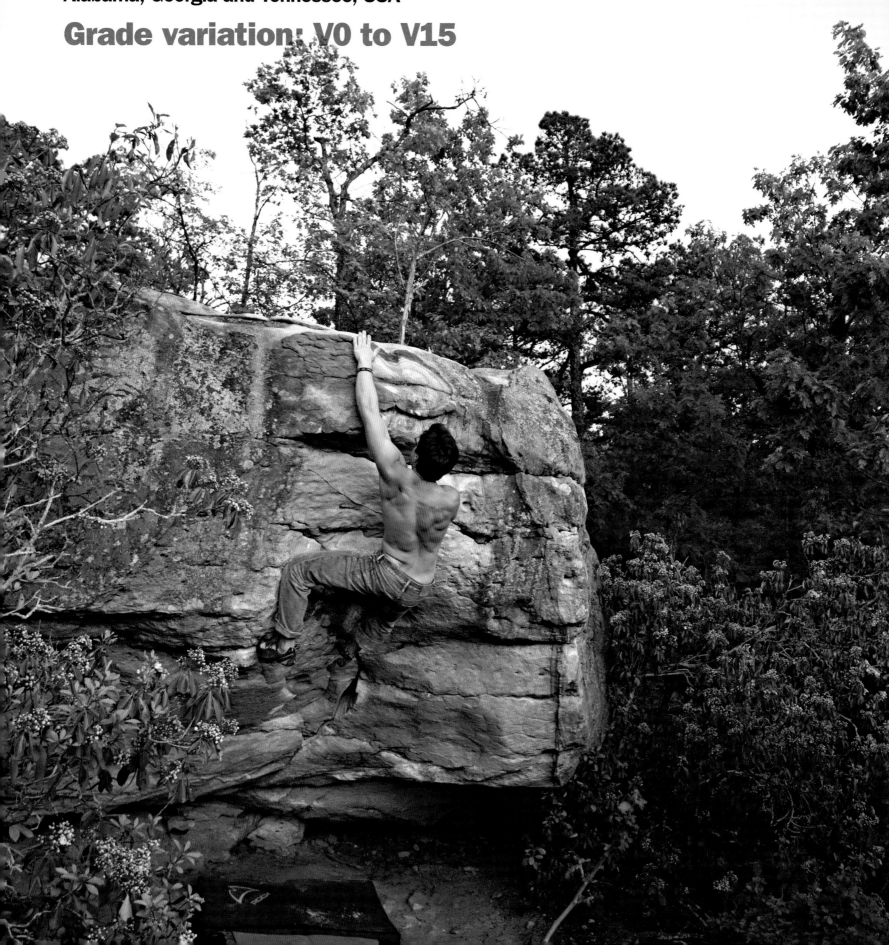

The Deep South
Alabama, Georgia and Tennessee, USA
Grade variation: V0 to V15

While the bouldering mecca of Fontainebleau, France, takes the crown for the most famous sandstone bouldering in the world, numerous areas in North America's 'Deep South' offer plenty of sandstone that is arguably just as good, with a much wider range of styles.

Commonly considered more brutal and basic than its European counterpart, American bouldering is often very physically demanding, with powerful moves through overhanging terrain on generally good holds. One of the exceptions to this rule is the bouldering of the southeast, especially the area of Horse Pens 40 in Alabama. Here the 'sloper' is king, and the boulders are often highly technical. Taxing footwork and intricate hand movements are the easiest ways to success, but remember to save some energy for the notoriously difficult 'top-outs', which are often the most demanding section of the climb.

With several major bouldering areas situated inside a two-hour triangle, the Deep South is a fantastic area for a climbing road trip. Petrol is cheap, accommodation plentiful, and that legendary southern hospitality is guaranteed to make your evenings just as memorable as your days. A classic road trip takes in the three states of Alabama, Georgia and Tennessee, the order really depending only on where you are coming from. Each state offers a slightly different style and feel, and will test climbers in different ways. Their respective hot spots are Horse Pens 40 (Alabama), Rocktown (Georgia) and Stone Fort (Tennessee).

The concentration of boulders is, in the main, high and the approach hikes are generally short. You can get a lot of climbing done in a short space of time, and it's normal to finish the day exhausted in both body and mind. People often say that the climbing in the Deep South is 'sandbagged', a term that climbers use when the grades given seem harder than they should be. This is usually due to a visiting climber's lack of familiarity with a certain rock type, making unusual holds and movements seem much harder than they actually are. Climbing in the Deep South definitely takes a certain amount of getting used to – yet just as with its French equivalent, Fontainebleau, if you take the time to learn and understand the many subtle details, you will later reap the rewards.

As with all sandstone, avoid climbing here after heavy rain as the rock becomes very delicate and is easily damaged. Also please consider that many of the areas in the Deep South are on private land, and climbers are only allowed to be there thanks to the good grace of the landowners. Please read and follow all the necessary rules, pay the required access fees and generally treat the area like it is your own home.

OPPOSITE: The classic overhanging corner of Redneck, one of the most sought-out problems at Horse Pens 40.

ABOVE: Nate Draughn on his first ascent of Jumby, V10.

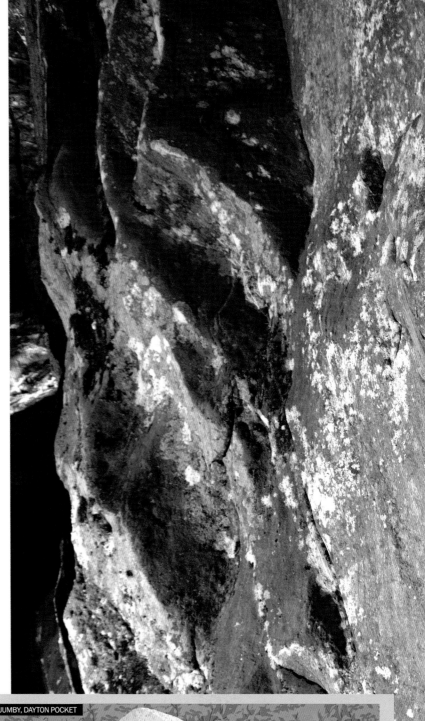

ABOVE: Eddie Gianelloni, stretching for the top on Latin for Daggers, V5.

RIGHT: One of the joys of making first ascents is taking the time to unlock the complicated beta. With so much unclimbed rock in the Deep South, this is a joy climbers find more often than usual.

Fact File The Deep South

TYPE OF CLIMB: Bouldering

TYPE OF ROCK: Sandstone

GRADE VARIATION: V0 to V15

CLIMB LENGTH: 2 to 10m

BEST TIME TO CLIMB: October to April

OTHER NOTABLE CLIMBS:
Golden Shower, V5; Bedwetters, V9

The Deep South Boulders

Stone Fort, Tennessee
Rocktown, Georgia
Horse Pens 40, Alabama

JUMBY, DAYTON POCKET

V10

South America

Patagonia **Argentina/Chile**

Grade variation: I to VII; 5.8 to 5.13; A1 to A4+; WI1 to WI7

Patagonia was once a far-away land, full of some of the most incredible mountain peaks imaginable but accessible only by a hardcore few. Climbing in Patagonia, specifically on the Chaltén Massif, was a place for mountaineers to escape to the wild, to pit their strength and wits against Mother Nature and the mountains, and generally to live a quiet life in peace. With some of the most changeable weather on the planet, Patagonian storms were the stuff of legend. Something that few had experienced and everyone wanted to avoid, they could appear from almost nothing, and in the space of a few hours change a pleasant day out into a life-threatening nightmare. Patagonia was the realm of mountain masters.

RIGHT: The view of part of the Chaltén Massif as you approach the town of El Chaltén from the south.

As time moved on, many aspects of Patagonian climbing became accessible to the regular mortal. Firstly, with the construction of El Chaltén, hotels, bars and restaurants meant that climbers now had a place to eat and sleep when they first arrived in the region, and somewhere to escape to during times of prolonged bad weather. With the rise of El Chaltén, the local infrastructure also improved. New roads and bridges changed what was once a long and harrowing journey into a pleasant drive, opening up Patagonia not only to climbing tourism but to all sorts of other outdoor pursuits.

The most important advance, however, was not physical but technological. With improvements in meteorological science and more accurate local equipment, scientists began to be able to accurately predict the fierce storms that often hammer the mountains of the Chaltén Massif, and subsequently the calm periods of good weather in between. Climbing in Patagonia is no longer a case of Russian roulette – climbers can now see upcoming weather windows several days in advance, allowing them not only to rest in preparation for a big push, but also to know by when exactly they need to be heading back down. This gives them a huge advantage over the early Patagonian pioneers – so much so that some purists claim that Patagonian climbing is not quite the adventure it once was. Wherever you stand on that, it's important to remember that the weather forecasts are not always perfect and that, when it hits, a Patagonian storm is as life threatening as it ever was.

RIGHT: The colourful town of El Chaltén.

BELOW: Patagonia goes on and on…

BELOW: A glacier flowing into a glacier lake at Cerro Torre, Patagonia.

The peaks of the Chaltén Massif are some of the most iconic mountains in the world, and just their names are enough to conjure up both hope and fear. The most iconic of all is arguably Cerro Torre, and the story of the first ascent of this majestic peak has more in common with a Hollywood movie than a major mountaineering achievement. In 1959, Cesare Maestri made the first ascent of the peak with his partner Toni Egger, who was tragically killed in an avalanche while the pair were descending, taking their camera and proof of the summit with him. Several years later, Maestri's claim was disputed after anomalies in his story came to light. Now in his eighties, Maestri still asserts his first-ascent claim, but a decision to reattempt the mountain in 1970 cast even further doubt, which was compounded by the style of his second climb. Maestri decided to attempt the feat – in total contrast to the pure ethics of regular mountaineering – carrying a 70-kilogram petrol generator and a hammer drill, slowly drilling his way up the mountain, bolt by bolt.

Maestri gave up his attempt at the infamous 'ice mushroom' that covers the summit of Cerro Torre, stating that the ice wasn't a real part of the mountain and that one day it would fall down. Despite the obvious questions raised by this, it was his total disregard for the accepted climbing style that offends climbers to this day.

In 2012 the young American/Canadian team of Hayden Kennedy and Jason Kruk caused a stir by removing more than 100 bolts from Maestri's Compressor Route, acting on their own instincts rather than via a collective, planned decision of the international climbing community. The pair were hailed by many as heroes, but there were others who were far less impressed, including the El Chaltén police force who arrested the pair on their return to town. By this point, despite its poor ethical origins, the Compressor Route had become the most popular way to the top of Cerro Torre, simply because it was the easiest. Kennedy and Kruk's decision to remove all the bolts was seen as elitist, denying less-gifted climbers the chance of reaching the top of the mountain.

Wherever you stand on that issue, the final chapter in the story of Cerro Torre and the Compressor Route is without a doubt one of the more impressive mountaineering feats of recent times. Just a few weeks after the bolts were removed, a young Austrian alpinist by the name of David Lama realized a three-year-long dream, and made the first free ascent of the mountain. Climbing from bottom to top in one push, free climbing every metre of rock and ice, Lama's ascent was even more impressive considering that the large quantity of bolts he had been planning to use for protection had recently been removed.

Cerro Torre is without doubt one of the most beautiful mountains in the world, yet its image has unfortunately been tarred by some divisive acts of mountaineering. With the bolts removed from the Compressor Route and a new, cutting-edge free route to the top, the climbing on Cerro Torre may finally match its beauty.

Fact File Patagonia

TYPE OF CLIMB: Adventure, multi-pitch, alpine, mountaineering

TYPE OF ROCK: Granite

GRADE VARIATION: I to VII; 5.8 to 5.13; A1 to A4+; WI1 to WI7

CLIMB LENGTH: Around 1,000m

BEST TIME TO CLIMB: October to April

OTHER NOTABLE CLIMBS: Los Ultimos Dias del Paraiso, 6c, A2

Cerro Torre

COMPRESSOR ROUTE, CERRO TORRE

VI, 5.11, A1, WI6
Free version 5.13b

Salto Angel **Venezuela**
Grade variation: E7

RIGHT: The Third Camp, 250 metres below the summit and the last to offer spacious room for climbers. Arnaud Petit took this picture as he was jugging on the rope on the last day of their 2006 ascent.

Fact File Salto Angel

TYPE OF CLIMB: Adventure, multi-pitch, trad

TYPE OF ROCK: Quartzite

GRADE VARIATION: E7

CLIMB LENGTH: 1,000m

BEST TIME TO CLIMB: April to October

OTHER NOTABLE CLIMBS: It is also possible to reach the top of Salto Angel with six days' hiking from Kamarata and an 18-abseil descent (300m left of the amphitheatre). Other possibilities for big-wall climbing in Venezuela include Roraima Tepui and Acopan Tepui, two classic destinations with much easier logistics.

SALTO ANGEL, VENEZUELA

The tepuis in Venezuela are a series of table-top mountains in the Guiana Highlands of South America. Surrounded by steep, quartzite cliffs up to 900 metres high, these walls are similar in stature to the famous El Capitan in California, the principal reference for big-wall climbing. The main difference here is that the approach required to reach the rock is much more than ten minutes from the road, and there is almost no fixed gear or rescue services in these remote mountains.

The most impressive tepui is the Salto Angel, a few metres left of the Angel Falls, the highest waterfall in the world at 979 metres. This wall has seen only four ascents in 25 years, and the fastest team spent 12 nights living and climbing on the wall. How can a low-altitude climb, in a friendly climate, be so hard to deal with?

Approaching the place is an entire and tiring journey in itself. Once you reach Ciudad Bolivar from Caracas, a two-hour flight takes you to Kamarata, from where you take a boat – if the native Pemon Indians are motivated to do so. After two days on an occasionally tricky river, you reach a base camp close to the mountain. Then a strenuous three-hour walk brings you to the base of a stunning amphitheatre. There is no other place in the world where you will have the feeling of being crushed by such an impressive wall. Everything is wet, grassy or overhanging, and the noise and the movement of the waterfall is enough to instil vertigo in even the most level-headed.

Climbing on the wet rock would not be a big deal if you didn't also have to struggle with loose rocks and poisonous spiders and centipedes. Placing your own protection and setting nearly every anchor also increases the difficulty and takes time. Of the 30 pitches you will have to solve, only a few are easy and half of them demand the very best from the very best climbers. In the middle of the route you will climb some big roofs that make a retreat extremely complicated if not impossible, adding to the drama of the climb. Near the top, a vertical pillar with no protection over 12 metres is a scary E7 that the last Brazilian expedition decided to aid climb, a decision that meant a full day's work. There is no let-up at the top of the route, either, as you are forced to pull on some fragile creepers that form a vertical 30-metre jungle, with the very real possibility that you will come face to face with a snake.

Of course the arrival at the top, a lost world full of endemic plants, beautiful eroded boulders and natural pools, is well worth the hard work. It is a place of true liberation.

For the foreseeable future, climbing the Salto Angel will remain a great adventure. People will have the chance to experience a climb where time seems to stop, a unique endeavour that you will wish lasted more than two weeks. To wake up in your portaledge, cut off from the world, facing the Amazonian jungle and enjoying the rainbows, the sea of clouds at sunrise and the thousands of flickers of light that are all gifts from the waterfall, is a unique experience.

After a few repetitions, the discovery of one or two less-demanding variants and the publication of a specific topo, this route, like other big achievements from a previous climbing era, will surely join the list of classics. When will it be climbed on-sight in one day? And why not soloed with a parachute on one's back? Each generation has its own challenges, but the Salto Angel will always remain a physical test and an incredible experience.

OPPOSITE: The sound of the waterfall is unrelenting, but after 12 days on the wall it becomes a part of you. Here, Stéphanie Bodet is jugging towards the summit on the last day of their 2006 ascent.

LEFT: One of the seven E7 pitches, a sustained overhang with loose rocks and tiny protection.

TOP & ABOVE: The first bivouac on the wall is rather small. The team spent six days here, as the climbers made little progress each day on the overhang above.

Europe

The Peak District England
Grade variation: Mod to E10; 3+ to 8B+

Three little words, 'the Peak District', carry a peculiar power throughout the climbing world, and not just for the British. For all climbers in the know, just the mention of the Peak District raises a curious smile, for even if they have never touched 'God's own rock' with their own hands, they have certainly heard the stories and have an idea of what it is all about.

The gritstone outcrops of Derbyshire and southern Yorkshire were first laid down as beds of sediment in the delta of an immense river during the Paleozoic period, around 300 million years ago. Revealed by erosion from the wind and rain, gritstone is a strong, smooth, yet incredibly grippy rock, and is home to some of the hardest, most dangerous trad climbs in the world.

Climbing first began here in the late 1800s as training for the 'greater ranges', as was the habit at the time. Perhaps the first person to climb for climbing's sake was J.W. Puttrell, who opened up routes such as Puttrell's Progress at Wharncliffe Crags and Sand Gully at Black Rocks. By the 1950s and 1960s, climbing had become a popular pastime in its own right, and its popularity has continued to grow.

British traditional climbing has a rather strict ethical code, and nowhere is it adhered more to than within the boundaries of the Peak District. What makes trad climbing unique is the lack of permanently fixed gear, unlike the majority of sport areas around the world. Instead of clipping onto bolts that have been glued into small holes drilled into the rock, a climber in the Peak District must use their own experience and cunning to place various forms of mechanical safety equipment into the features left by Mother Nature herself. Not only does this approach leave the climber 100-per-cent responsible for their own safety, it also means that certain routes, light on helpful holes and cracks, can have little in the way of protection, or even none at all.

OPPOSITE: The first ascent of The Groove by James Pearson.

Fact File The Peak District

TYPE OF CLIMB: Trad, bouldering

TYPE OF ROCK: Gritstone

GRADE VARIATION: Mod to E10; 3+ to 8B+

CLIMB LENGTH: 2 to 15m

BEST TIME TO CLIMB: October to April

OTHER NOTABLE CLIMBS: Suicide Wall, HVS; Archangel, E3; Master's Edge, E7

① The Groove, E10, 7b   ③ Fern Hill, E2, 5c
② Nutcracker, E3, 5c   ④ Owl Gully, VD

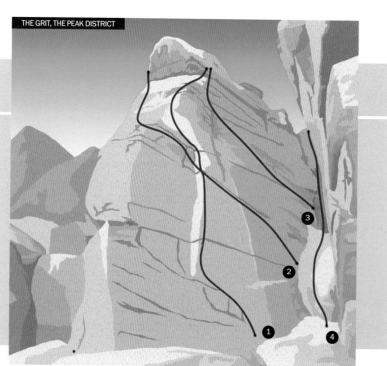

THE GRIT, THE PEAK DISTRICT

Gritstone has an unusually high degree of friction, meaning that one can hold handholds and push on footholds that would be simply impossible on other forms of rock. Climbing on gritstone is incredibly technically demanding, but subtle shifts in one's body position can change a seemingly impossible problem into a walk in the park. It is for this very reason that gritstone can be incredibly frustrating for visiting climbers during their first days – and utterly addictive by the end of the week. Very few people visit 'the grit' only once in their life, despite the often horrendous yet typical British weather.

Gritstone is full of classic, visually appealing routes at every grade, but one that stands out above the others in terms of both difficulty and looks is The Groove at Cratcliffe Tor. For many years, this almost sculpted feature in the middle of a beautiful grey wall was one of the most sought-after, unclimbed lines in the Peak District. Nobody had been able to solve its problems, until one day in 2008, a creative, almost conceptual sequence of moves proved to be the key, and opened the door to one of the most beautiful climbs in the country.

Gritstone has a character all of its own, and climbing on it is far more on its terms than yours. There will be days when everything feels easy, and days when you can barely leave the floor. It is a serious place to go climbing, and one that its history of tragedies reinforces. It's important, as ever, to understand how your own ability stacks up against the level of the route, but the most important thing of all is respect. Listen to the rock and play by its rules.

RIGHT: James returns to The End of the Affair (E8, 6b) at Curbar Edge in the Peak District. He had made the first onsight ascent of this route on a previous visit.

Nesscliffe
Shropshire, England
Grade variation: VS to E9

Despite being relatively well frequented by local and international climbers alike, Nesscliffe remains a curiously secret spot on the UK traditional climbing scene. Located just north of the River Severn as it meanders past Shrewsbury, it is set apart from other, more popular venues such as the Peak District and north Wales, and therefore remains relatively unspoilt. A brilliant cliff of red and brown sandstone, it has some of the best lines in Great Britain.

The cliff offers a varied series of challenges for every climber, with routes at either end of both the difficulty and danger spectrums. The sandstone of Nesscliffe can be very soft, and has a tendency to appear far easier than it actually is. Take extra care with smears and slopers, as they can be slippery and sandy, and pay particular attention to your gear placements – what seems solid at first can sometimes pull out unexpectedly during a fall.

Nesscliffe was once a working sandstone quarry, and traces of ancient tools, as well as engravings from the Victorian workers, can still be seen to this day. The quarrying process morphed the typically smooth contours of the natural sandstone face into an incredibly geometric, angular form, and it is these never-ending corners and arêtes that make Nesscliffe so interesting for climbers today.

Typically, routes at Nesscliffe are either bold and precarious or safe and sustained. The delicate arêtes offer little in the form of protection, whereas the corners often follow deep cracks. In more recent years, climbers have begun to venture out onto the blank faces in between, and these days it is here that the cliff's hardest challenges can be found. These face routes offer an interesting mix of the two styles, somehow thuggish but at the same time technical. They are often protected by a series of curious *in-situ* protection points such as nails and parts of cars, giving the routes more of a sport-climbing feel. Yet unlike the typical bolts and pitons normally used, these seem to be whatever the first climber could find in his shed at the time.

Two of Nescliffe's most sought-after climbs show off the variety of approaches perfectly. Wildly different in character, yet on paper fairly similar, My Piano (E8, 6b) and Une Jeune Fille 90 Ans ('A Young Girl in Her 90s'; E8, 6c) are two exciting routes that will challenge both courage and technique. Despite their relative proximity and grade, the two routes could not be further apart in style and approach. While My Piano is a bold and dangerous undertaking, in which falling off is simply not an option, Un Jeune Fille 90 Ans is technical to the extreme, yet relatively well protected in its more difficult sections.

Climbing My Piano requires complete control of one's body and mastery of one's mind. Every movement should be static, wiping off the possible grains of sand on each hold before pulling on it to avoid any nasty surprises, and checking that your protection is perfectly placed and secure. Une Jeune Fille 90 Ans, on the other hand, will be a battle with your physical boundaries, demanding 100 per cent of your technical capacity yet in a situation where a mistake or fatigue is less likely to be life threatening. This diversity is one of the most exciting aspects of the UK's traditional climbing scene, and is one of the reasons that Nescliffe tempts even those climbers 'in the know' to come back time and time again.

ABOVE: A Thousand Setting Suns, E9.
OPPOSITE: Look closely and you may spot some of Nesscliffe's curious *in-situ* protection.

NEXT PAGE: My Piano, the elegant, classic, yet dangerous E8.

Fact File Nesscliffe

TYPE OF CLIMB: Trad

TYPE OF ROCK: Quarried sandstone

GRADE VARIATION: VS to E9

CLIMB LENGTH: 25m

BEST TIME TO CLIMB: Spring and autumn

OTHER NOTABLE CLIMBS: A Thousand
Setting Suns, E9; YuKan 2, E7

NESSCLIFFE, SHROPSHIRE

Nesscliffe

E8　　　E2

1 My Piano, E8, 6b

2 Red Square, E2, 5b

The Slate Llanberis, Wales
Grade variation: VDiff to E8; 4+ to 9a

The climber is always on the search for rock with great texture and a combination of movements that will make a route unique and demanding. Today, with much of the world climbed and mapped, what comes to mind when wishing for a new challenge and a new place to discover – a virgin cliff with steep profiles, full of difficult routes? Forget the stereotypes and turn the wheel of time backwards, before climbers had stereotypes to follow or avoid, and the slate was blank.

Slate? Indeed, The Slate. Not a virgin crag, but quite the opposite: immense holes dug by men in centuries past. The slate quarries in Llanberis, Wales, have been exploited for roofing material since the end of the 18th century, and the immense pits they created revealed to the air rocks that would otherwise have stayed buried. Once the good slate had all been used, the pits left behind were vast and intricate – and to a modern climber's eye, they constitute perfect slabby walls.

In the 1960s, the Dinorwic Quarry near Llanberis, once the second-largest slate quarry in the world, was abandoned. After years of sometimes unplanned quarrying, it had become too difficult and too dangerous to continue work without risking the old piles sliding into the holes. In addition, cheaper slate from China and Spain had driven Welsh slate out of the market. From a workforce of 3,000 men at its high point – quarrying, cutting slates, exploding the rock and transporting it – the quarry was suddenly empty.

Traditionally, shiny and slippery slate would never appeal to a climber as a rock with the ability to create good challenges. On the other hand, generations of quarrymen had already been using ropes to access all the levels, often scrambling and climbing to reach them. It should be no surprise, then, that with the emerging technology in climbing equipment – ropes, harnesses, carabiners – people would come back to the quarries and climb, but this time without any goal other than the challenge.

The Slate has become a climbing sanctuary. What was home to intense labour has turned into a new theatre of sport, full of daring propositions and sometimes absurd danger. Routes that carry a very British humour to their names – Dawes of Perception, Raped by Affection – are intricate and bold. They are by no means the most physically demanding climbs, but they are certainly some of the most daring. Here, adrenaline and risk are high. The height of the cavernous walls and the slippery nature of slate mean that danger is always near.

Behind every historical route there is a historical climber, and for Welsh slate climbing there are two men whose routes are as formidable as their own rivalry – John Redhead and Johnny Dawes. These two legendary climbers have a near-inexplicable view on the purpose of life: they have simply lived for climbing, daring to compete and to complete the impossible, and in so doing they have contributed to the unique spirit of The Slate's routes.

If you had to pick only one route out of the multitude within The Slate, it would have to be The Quarryman. This four-pitch, semi-bolted route stands as the most famous of them all, mainly because of the legendary pitch three, known as The Groove. On this tricky route, you find yourself shuffling up a glassy corner with holds so small that even the eye doesn't spot them: you pass your hand over the slate, and when your fingers feel the imperfection, you decide that this will become a foothold. Of course, it was only Johnny Dawes who could have had the vision of a route in this improbable corner of blank rock. Dawes' innate talent for the sport allowed him to see routes where none exist. And as per his style, it is therefore no wonder that the solutions to the hardest sections are movements that you would more expect to see in a circus. Particularly notable is his 'iron cross' move, which sees both arms spread between both walls of the corner, whilst balancing his legs in the air and swinging to create enough momentum to bring them high enough to reach a foothold nearly a metre further away. Crazy? This is Johnny Dawes. And this is The Slate.

OPPOSITE: The near perfection of a slate slab demands perfect footwork.

Fact File The Slate

TYPE OF CLIMB: Trad or sport, but with a very 'traddy' spirit

TYPE OF ROCK: Slate

GRADE VARIATION: VDiff to E8; 4+ to 9a

CLIMB LENGTH: 10 to 100m

BEST TIME TO CLIMB: Spring and autumn

OTHER NOTABLE CLIMBS: Poetry Pink, E4; The Meltdown, 9a; Comes the Dervish, E3

Llanberis

THE QUARRYMAN, THE SLATE

E8

E8

Abseil approach from ledge

E5

E6

Scramble approach from tunnels

RIGHT: Caroline Ciavaldini on Swan Hunter at the Looning the Tube area. Some of the routes on this slab start by traversing the decaying metal tube. Spice is always on the menu here!

LEFT: Caroline climbing The Groove pitch on The Quarryman.

TOP & ABOVE: Two glass-like faces, two different techniques, one goal: UP, somehow!

St Govan's Pembrokeshire, Wales
Grade variation: Difficult to E10

Fact File St Govan's

TYPE OF CLIMB: Trad

TYPE OF ROCK: Limestone

GRADE VARIATION: Difficult to E10

CLIMB LENGTH: 15 to 45m

BEST TIME TO CLIMB: All year round

OTHER NOTABLE CLIMBS: Mysteries, E3;
Something's Burning, E9

St Govan's

1 Point Blank, E8, 6c   3 Muy Caliente, E10, 6c

2 From a Distance, E7, 6b   4 Ghost Train, E6, 6b

STENNIS FORD, ST GOVAN'S

LEFT: Yuji Hirayama coils his ropes after his first day climbing in Pembrokeshire.

Walking onto St Govan's Range East for the first time, you might be surprised to learn that it is one of the UK's premier traditional climbing areas, world famous for its compact, fractured limestone and amazingly varied routes. At first glance, there is nothing here that resembles 'rock' in the slightest – just endless flat, grassy pastures, dotted by the occasional sheep or decaying tank track. Be very careful, though, as suddenly the flat, green fields drop 30 vertical metres to the crashing sea below. This is Pembrokeshire and British sea-cliff climbing at its very best, and climbers from all around the world flock here every summer to test their fingers and their nerves.

Climbing here comes in all forms, from long, bold slabs to technical, brutal finger cracks, but for the most part it is well protected and relatively simple. The Pembrokeshire coast is often referred to as having trad climbing for sport climbers – if you have the fitness and know-how to wiggle in small 'wires', then you're going to love it here. There is something magically intimidating about descending by abseil to your chosen route, giant waves pounding over the rocky shore below, and knowing that the only way back out is to succeed on your challenge for the day. There is no question about it – climbing in Pembrokeshire is committing, far more so than some of the other popular UK trad venues. But it is also very rewarding, and you finish each and every day with a real sense of achievement.

One of the first main areas any visiting climber will see is the wide-open chasm of Stennis Ford. Although home to some of the hardest routes Pembrokeshire has to offer, Stennis should not be thought of as only an elite-level crag. While it is true that there are no 'easy' routes here, there are plenty of classic E3s, 4s and 5s, with routes such as Mysteries and Suspense being some of the best of their grade in the country. At the extreme end of the difficulty spectrum – and currently the only route of this level to have ever been climbed without the security of 'top rope' practise – is Muy Caliente (E10/6c). This imposing, dangerous route takes a bold and direct line up one of the blankest faces around, packing in many difficult and tiring movements and with very little in the way of reliable protection. Climbing a route such as Muy Caliente requires total commitment and an acceptance that any mistake could be fatal. Routes like this are not for the faint hearted, yet the total immersion in the moment that they offer is what drives climbers to tackle its challenge.

RIGHT: James Pearson on the first and
only ground-up ascent of Muy Caliente.

James Pearson climbed it in 2012. 'Muy Caliente has to be the most fun, dangerous route in the UK,' he says. 'It's just brilliant. After climbing the first easy ten metres up to a nest of good gear, you bust it out up a gently overhanging wall, with every move taking you further and further away from your protection. The moves are fun, the rock is fantastic and everything flows perfectly. It's easy to lose yourself in the moment and forget that a fall from the last few moves on this section will likely see you in pieces on the rocky beach below. It is bold trad at its best – total immersion!'

A large percentage of the south Pembrokeshire coastline is covered by active military firing ranges, and this presents a double-edged sword. On the one hand, the beautiful Welsh landscape is kept well preserved, untouched by modern construction, but on the other hand, the general public can only enjoy access to this incredible part of the world on certain days and at certain times. Add to that the enormous tidal range, one of the biggest in the world (up to 10 metres), and it can sometimes quite literally be impossible to go climbing on the sea cliffs in this area. That being said, whatever the reason for visiting, and despite all the complications, once a climber has tasted a little of what Pembrokeshire has to offer, they will undoubtedly come back for more.

ABOVE LEFT: James making the first ascent of Do You Know Where Your Children Are, E9.

ABOVE CENTRE: Mother Cary's Kitchen is home to some of the steepest routes around. The water makes you feel safe, but don't relax: one metre of water will never ease your fall!

ABOVE RIGHT: Caroline takes her very first big trad fall, on Point Blank, E8.

Céüse Hautes-Alpes, France
Grade variation: 5+ to 9a+

What do climbers think of when they hear the word 'Céüse'? The most famous cliff in France, some would even argue that it's the best cliff in the world. It is home to Biographie, graded 9a+ and one of the hardest routes in the world in its time, a route freed by the living legend, Chris Sharma, in 2001.

In summer, a campsite full of climbers sits at the bottom of an immense face of grey limestone, a huge cliff that rests like a hat forming the top of the mountain. It's impossible to miss Céüse; it calls to you from the valley below. It is the symbol of a milestone in sport-climbing history, and its historical significance has made it a social rendezvous for climbers from all over the world. Their coloured tents and eager hands flock to it throughout the summer.

But there is also another Céüse. It is still wild and nearly empty, and just a short walk on from the main attraction. Here you will find another epic wall with discoveries beckoning: this is the Grande Face.

Here, you are all alone on top of the mountain, the city of Gap far away on the horizon. Above you are 100 metres of pure, grey limestone. The most famous route up is Natilik. An historical route, it was opened in 1980 by two great French climbers, Jean-Christophe Lafaille and Philippe Macle. Both have sadly died in their pursuit of climbing, but these two pioneers leave behind them some incredible records, one of which is the beautiful Natilik.

As you stand on the starting platform and tilt your head up, all you can see is a gigantic roof around 60 metres up. Even the head wall is hidden from you, and it seems impossible that a 6b route could pass here.

It begins quite typically, up a weakness in the crag. The climbing is easy but wild, with only a few hard-to-spot bolts showing you the way up. It is essential to have friends and nuts in between the bolts: you are out of the sport-climbing kingdom here. After two pitches, the key to the mystery reveals itself: a giant horizontal crack that allows you to pass the huge roof without hanging on your arms. After that, it's a 'simple' matter of crawling for 20 metres in the crack to join the head wall. Your body will be precariously jammed inside, one leg hanging in space and your head out, facing the air. Underneath you, the view stretches to the foothills of the Alps. The sun, if it's out, will catch the crag just at the moment you get off the crack, with the head wall above you glistening like the gem the route is.

LEFT: Comfortable belays – one of the features of a great route.

RIGHT: Caroline on the third pitch, a 20-metre crawl along the crack that allows you to pass the immense roof without really using your arms.

Just one more pitch remains before the route leads you into an extremely 'airy' section. Look down at the floor sweeping away to the valley – a view that for many is vertigo inducing. At the top, you reach a plateau shared only with birds. This small, grassy-meadow area is only accessible via the multi-pitch routes of La Grande Face, on the top of the mighty Céüse. A climber's path will lead you down, but here you are on top of the world. This is Céüse.

LEFT: The city of Gap in the background, illuminated by the morning sun.

NATILIK, LA GRANDE FACE, CÉÜSE

Descend on rappel or hike down

Pitch 4 – 8a

Pitch 3 – 5

Pitch 2 – 6b

Pitch 1 – 6a+

Fact File Céüse

TYPE OF CLIMB: Sport, multi-pitch

TYPE OF ROCK: Limestone

GRADE VARIATION: 5+ to 9a+

CLIMB LENGTH: 15 to 100m

BEST TIME TO CLIMB: May to October

OTHER NOTABLE CLIMBS: La Petite Illusion, 7a+; Biographie, 9a+

Céüse

Grand Capucin
Mont Blanc Massif, France
Grade variation: 4+ to 8b

If alpinism is about going up a snowy mountain and hoping to reach the summit, then climbing is about going up a rocky face and hoping to reach its top. Climbing was actually born as a training activity for alpinists, and of course both sports are intertwined where rock meets ice. On the Mont Blanc Massif, at nearly 4,000 metres of altitude,

climbing becomes alpinism. As a climber, you can try something you know nothing about – choose an approach on crampons instead of the usual hike to the crag; cross a glacier to reach a rocky face that is much higher than you are familiar with; and then climb as you would in your normal playground ... with a little extra element: the altitude.

LEFT: Caroline on the second-to-last pitch of the Voie Petit – perfect alpine granite.

Fact File Grand Capucin

TYPE OF CLIMB: Alpine-altitude multi-pitch

TYPE OF ROCK: Granite

GRADE VARIATION: 4+ to 8b

CLIMB LENGTH: 450m

BEST TIME TO CLIMB: Summer

OTHER NOTABLE CLIMBS: La Voie des Suisses, 6b; Voie Bonatti, 7a+

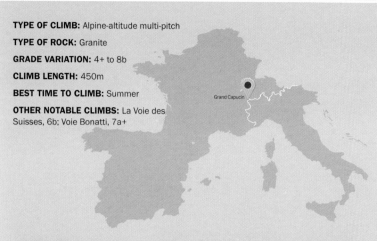

Grand Capucin

THE VOIE PETIT, GRAND CAPUCIN

6a
6b
7b+
6c
8a
5c
3c
7b+
7c+
8b
6b+
6b
7b
6a

Climbing on the Grand Capucin, a rock pinnacle and one of the most vertical peaks of the Mont Blanc Massif, is all about granite climbing technique and rope management. But it is just as imperative to be astute about the weather, how to endure a cold climate, the altitude and the natural feeling of fear that these induce. It is also about being transported to a grey and white, silent world.

The Grand Capucin is home to some classical routes, the first of them being the sacred Voie Bonatti, opened by Walter Bonatti in 1951. It is 7a+ on paper, but paper isn't really relevant here. This is 'adventurous terrain', as you would say in French, and a grade of 7a is a very serious challenge when the bolts become pitons or natural protection.

There are younger routes, of course, a new generation of routes and their climbers. One such, the Voie Petit, is the hardest route on the Grand Capucin. Graded 8b max, it was opened in 1997 by Arnaud Petit with Stéphanie Bodet, Pascal Gaudin and Jean-Paul Petit. Arnaud was searching for some hard climbing in the Alps, and seeing the virgin rock remaining on the Grand Capucin, he began to dream of a route. Of course, opening such a difficult route at that altitude is an extraordinary effort and, following the alpine tradition, Arnaud aimed to place as few bolts as possible in the rock, relying where possible on temporary protection. The feat took him and his team a full summer to finally complete. The route got its name as a nod to the old fashion of naming routes after the person who opened it, but at that point no one had managed to free climb it. It was a challenge offered to the whole climbing world. It comprises 13 pitches, including one 8b, one 8a and one 7c+, demanding the skills of a gifted sport climber. Yet with few bolts in each pitch, any aspiring climber would need the trad and alpine experience to go with it.

Only in 2005 did Alex Huber free the route, followed by Arnaud and other legendary climbers. It was given the grade of 8b max, the hardest climb currently existing in the French Alps at that altitude.

If you decide to take on the route, the adventure will start pretty smoothly via a telepherique ride up to the refuge of Torino. You get out and you are in the snow, with the Dent du Géant, a monunental rocky tooth, in front of you. From there you have to cross the Glacier du Géant on crampons with ropes, ice axes and ice screws – in case you fall into a crevasse – until you arrive in a semi-circle of peaks. The snow glitters in the sun and the grey of the granite becomes orange. The Petit Capucin (3,693 metres) and the Grand Capucin (3,838 metres) tower above you, the most vertical peaks around and 450 metres higher than the frozen plain. A night camping at its foot, on the ice, will allow you the early start needed to attempt the Voie Petit. What is so extraordinary about this route is that quality combined with beauty is extremely hard to find. Did Arnaud get lucky, or was he already such a talented 'rock finder' when he was 20 years old? The route is there as his testimony, the line going up the proud arête to the summit. The crux pitch is simply breathtaking, with first a technical dihedral, the roof cut by a single crack, that just about allows you to pass until you are back on vertical ground. It is the easier upper pitches, however – the 6b arête with only air below you, and the 6a on perfect weathered granite – that will completely charm you.

The young climber loves rock in all its forms, albeit with the slight sense that some routes feel better than others. With experience, more details stand out and the climber becomes an expert diner: the grain of the rock, the shape of the holds, the surprise of the sequence. The Voie Petit deserves a place in any three-star Michelin guide.

TOP: The approach will require crampons!
ABOVE: Camping on ice at the bottom of the Grand Capucin makes for a cold early start.

OPPOSITE: Caroline on the lower groove of the crux pitch, a technical section that demands precision and concentration.

Les Calanques Marseilles, France
Grade variation: 4+ to 9a

RIGHT: Quite a location! Perfect orange limestone, turquoise water and the Calanque of Cassis in the background.

The second-biggest city in France after Paris, Marseille has its own very distinctive style. One of its biggest attractions is the sun-soaked national park of the Calanques. Stretching out from the magnificent blue of the Mediterranean Sea, the Parc National des Calanques stretches for 520 square kilometres of land and sea, its high, limestone rocks towering out of the turquoise waters. Thanks to their protected status the Calanques have remained wild, with only the odd quietly floating boat or kayak, helping to take walkers and climbers to its trickier patches, interrupting its wilderness.

This special spot was made famous in the climbing world by the hard sport-crags of La Grotte de l'Hermite (The Hermit Cave) and l'Ours (The Bear), among others. Most of these were developed and chipped by climbers (using a drill and hammer to manufacture holds), making use of the steep, often horizontal rock faces to create physical, athletic routes. This practice was seen as a way to create new challenges, and was particularly common during the 1990s. Though it is no longer the common approach to creating new climbs, these remain as historic routes that still attract and demand our attention. In particular, Rastata (8b), and Les Liaisons Dangereuses (8b) stand as testimony to the surge of climbing expertise in France during the 1990s, and have become an integral part of France's climbing heritage. At this time, France was seen to have some of the hardest routes on Earth and the best climbers pushing the sport to new levels.

Today, several decades on from this pioneering era, Les Calanques is still very much worth discovering. Most now go for the allure of the multi-pitches. Here you can climb straight over the sea in three, four or five pitches, basking in the Marseille sun and taking in the magnificence of the white cliffs that are the treasure of Calanques. When you reach the summit, you can see all the way to Cassis and Marseille.

With technology and climbing reaching new heights, the multi-pitches are now considered accessible. If you are looking for more adrenaline, there are a few deep-water solo crags that have been opened in recent

LEFT: Sea and sun – James Pearson posing for the photographer on one of the Calanques' easy yet exposed multi-pitches.

Fact File Les Calanques

TYPE OF CLIMB: Sport, multi-pitch

TYPE OF ROCK: Limestone

GRADE VARIATION: 4+ to 9a

CLIMB LENGTH: 20 to 150m

BEST TIME TO CLIMB: Autumn to spring

OTHER NOTABLE CLIMBS: Les Dents de la Mer, 6b+; Armata Calanca, 6c; UFO, 8c

Les Calanques

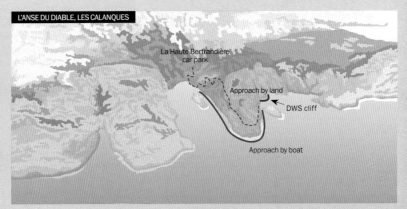

L'ANSE DU DIABLE, LES CALANQUES

La Haute Bertrandière car park

Approach by land

DWS cliff

Approach by boat

years by Vincent Albrand, founder and owner of Grimper climbing gyms. Albrand was one of the top climbers of his era and, in his own quiet and gentle style, opened some ferocious climbs at l'Anse du Diable (The Bay of the Devil). 'We decided to open the routes without cleaning them before starting from sea level, because it seemed like a better style,' Albrand explains.

To get to this spot you have to gain access from the water, either by kayak or a small dingy, to allow you to get as close as possible to the edge of the rock. From here you step out of your boat in time with the wave's retreat and quickly climb one or two movements before the wave comes back. From then onwards, or perhaps that should be upwards, it's just you and the rock. The rock is made up of what seem like endless round pebbles, from the size of a pigeon's egg up to that of a football,

all imprisoned in a geological matrix. Be warned, though, that despite their solid appearance, some of these pebbles are not as trapped as you might think and can easily slip out. It is not unusual to see a surprised climber falling off straight into the sea, with a pebble still in their hand.

Sometimes the sea is so warm that jellyfish swim next to the shore, giving your adventure an added edge of peril. Vincent Albrand would tell you not to worry – 'They don't hurt that much.'

ABOVE: The routes usually top out close to the road, and sometimes right next to your car.

OPPOSITE: In the Calanques, most of the time you abseil first before climbing. You had better be sure you'll be able to climb back up!

Fontainebleau Paris, France
Grade variation: 3+ to 8C+

Just south of Paris, easily accessible by local transport, is the rather unassuming forest of Fontainebleau. Unassuming it may be, but it is home – for most climbers – to the best bouldering on Earth.

In the middle of the forest, sandstone boulders seem to be floating on a sea of sand. The rocks are made up of the most unique quality of fine sandstone, a geological heritage of the *bassin parisien* – a shallow water basin where sand has been deposited for millions of years. As the climate changed and water retreated, the most fragile parts of the soft sand eroded, leaving a series of boulders dotted through the forest. The more you climb, the more you marvel at the quality of the rock, and the more you learn to appreciate its grain.

Fontainebleau is a marvel of nature, a gift to all mountain lovers stuck in the metropolis. Bouldering was born here, as Parisian climbers searched for rock to train on ahead of their summer trips to Chamonix. As the sport has progressed, with new tools creating new techniques, this place has only improved. Higher, harder – the game continues as the sport and boulders continue to evolve.

BELOW LEFT: The sandstone kingdom! Fontainebleau is a must-visit area in the climbing world for the quality of its rock.

BELOW: Caroline desperately searching for the way on Science Friction.

The main question you'll find yourself asking at Fontainbleau is how to choose only one boulder – four little metres of climbing – within an immense forest of rock. One test piece, a classic, as climbers would say, is Science Friction, 6a. On this perfect slab in Apremont, only the slight change of colour of the rock made by a passing climber will show you the 'holds', such as they are. Vague bumps, tiny imperfections are all you can push on with your feet, expecting every second to plunge back to the forest floor. Next to no hands and fewer than six foot movements – these are the boulder's requirements. It is a true test of balance and friction, and one where you can only end up atop the boulder if you have been perfect. No matter what your level is on overhangs, no matter how much you have trained indoors, Science Friction is always able to resist an impatient climber. Learn to pull, to try hard, to train – but first of all, learn to place and trust your feet.

Over the past few years, a young climber called Charles Albert has been busy in the forests of Fontainebleau. He has long, dark hair, a red bandana and a little piece of cloth to clean his feet. He has no climbing shoes, and wanders barefoot through the forest without a crash pad or chalk. You could believe that you have just met Mowgli from *The Jungle Book*, except that he climbs on rock instead of trees. Albert realized years ago that he climbed better using the strength of his toes, crimping edges and toe hooking by flexing rather than with his feet imprisoned in shoes. He feels his way around the boulders and his unique approach has enabled him to achieve more than many older climbers in this spot. Climbing grades indicate how incredible he is – La Valse aux Adieux, 8C; L'Alchimiste, 8B+ ... but just watching him is even better. Albert is not even 20 years old, but he's decided to follow his own path, to create his own climbing rules. The reason for this is quite simple: 'When I was 16, I bought a pair of climbing shoes just before going on holiday,' he says. 'When I came back home to climb, the shoes were too small. So I decided I would climb without shoes.' And why not? His style, approach and technique are what climbing is all about: being free. And where better to do that than in the best bouldering playground there is.

LEFT: James using the one and only handhold on Science Friction.

Fact File Fontainebleau

TYPE OF CLIMB: Bouldering

TYPE OF ROCK: Sandstone

GRADE VARIATION: 3+ to 8C+ – everything from easy to impossible; this is where bouldering was born

CLIMB LENGTH: Less than 10m

BEST TIME TO CLIMB: Winter for friction, spring and autumn for leisure

OTHER NOTABLE CLIMBS: Marie Rose, 6B; Carnage, 7B+; The Big Island, 8C

Fontainebleau

SCIENCE FRICTION, APREMONT, FONTAINEBLEAU

6A

BELOW: James on Alexia de Galaxia, one of the best routes at La Pedriza.

La Pedriza Madrid, Spain
Grade variation: 3+ to 8B+

In most major climbing destinations, a community of local climbers is already established. Metéora, the Peak District, The Slate, Zillertal: they all have their aficionados, climbers born and bred there or sometimes adopted. The community knows all the crags and excels at the style.

Of course, on the 'modern' overhanging limestone crags, the style is commonly known, and you can go from one area to another without being hugely surprised. But there are other places, nothing like those you have ever seen before, where one's first days of climbing seem like learning a new sport. The rock is different and the style is different. Is it the rock that dictates the style? Or the other way around – the bolter who prints his style to a route?

La Pedriza, only forty minutes from Madrid, appears as if from a dream when you turn a corner on the road from the city: granite domes fill the horizon. It is a national park where climbing has been allowed because it was there before anything else. Such a long history of climbing on such

atypically angled slabs has produced generations of technical masters. They find footholds where no one else would.

The granite of La Pedriza is exceptionally compact, which allows the climber to push the friction challenge to the extreme. Sixty-degree slabs, and only a few smears; a piece of rock becomes a hold because you have decided that it will be one. One crystal becomes a thumb, and as soon as you are gone and your chalk mark is erased by the rain or the wind, that crystal is just a crystal again. It is a piece of rock that is perfect, infinite, and the climber has to learn to become perfect too, to stay on their feet.

Fact File La Pedriza

TYPE OF CLIMB: Sport, trad, multi-pitch

TYPE OF ROCK: Granite

GRADE VARIATION: 3+ to 8B+

CLIMB LENGTH: 2 to 150m

BEST TIME TO CLIMB: European winter

OTHER NOTABLE CLIMBS: Inuit, 8b+; Alexia de Galaxia, 8a+

La Pedriza

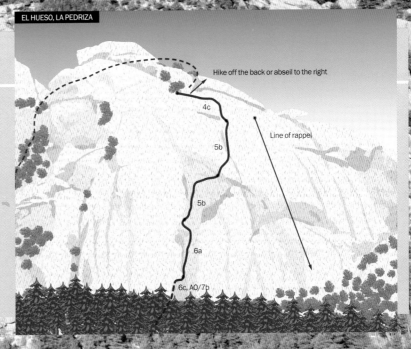

EL HUESO, LA PEDRIZA

Hike off the back or abseil to the right

4c

5b

Line of rappel

5b

6a

6c, AO/7b

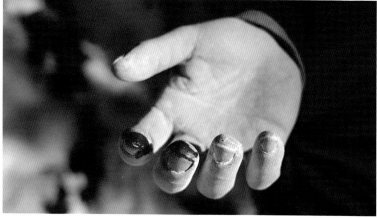

El Hueso ('The Bone') is arguably the most famous of the many multi-pitches. It has a miraculous shape that allows you to follow its narrow stretch in an arch, detached from the main face by only one metre. Here is a sight that has to be seen, the arc continuing for over 60 metres. It is an easy and bolted climb, but the far-away bolts will give you plenty of testing times and interesting emotions. Perched on El Hueso at the belay point, studying the face neighbouring your arch of rock, you have to convince yourself that the floor under you isn't balancing in the wind. Look on the other side and its fragility is even more pronounced, the arch getting finer and finer as it goes up; one day, erosion and gravity will bring El Hueso down, but for now, the miracle lives on.

On the hardest section (6a in the book, but there is a world behind a grade), the climber will face a compact granite slab with next to no imperfections. At first, it looks absolutely impossible. You will have to trust a vague bulge for your hand, use it to keep your balance and place your foot in the next slight bulge or hollow, believing that the friction between rubber and rock will be enough to stick. The game continues, on and on, every breath taken with precaution to minimize the pressure changes under your feet as you hope that the next, easier, section will arrive soon.

The more time you spend on La Pedriza's technical rock, the more you start to learn its essential lessons. Little by little you start to understand the rock; your squinting, searching eyes get faster at spotting the crystal holds and your mind and heart begin to learn the pace of granite. Its blank-looking sections are no longer points where it looks as if you will slide and scratch yourself, but canvases where you will create your own way across.

La Pedriza is the ultimate technical rock. Its magic lies in its endless ability to teach the climber, new or old, beginner or experienced: it is not about strength, but about precision and trust.

Its famous rocks will implore you back. It isn't a promise, it is a certitude, because in La Pedriza you will always be able to climb, learn and contemplate, no matter how old you get.

TOP: From multi-pitch to boulders, you can find it all in La Pedriza.
ABOVE LEFT: Granite and its crystals have consequences: sometimes you can lose a good bit of skin while pulling on a sharp hold.

OPPOSITE: Talo Martin in action – perfect footwork and bouldering flexibility.

Roca Verde Asturias, Spain
Grade variation: 3+ to 8C

A combination of stable weather and incredible rock has always made Spain a popular destination for the avid climber, and as the sport has grown over the past few years, Spain has benefited from the rise in holiday climbing. The routes are well bolted, there are many different areas and styles, and the local climbers are almost always in good spirits. Every November, as the season turns from summer to autumn, thousands of climbers travel south on their seasonal migration.

For many, Spain is the sport-climbing centre of the world. A large country – over twice the size of the UK – it is littered with alluring destinations, almost giving the sense that there is an unlimited amount of rock. Despite being incredibly popular, for those climbers who enjoy quieter crags, there are still plenty of less well-known spots to explore that are just as good as the famous ones that attract a multitude of climbers.

To be technically correct, the 'Spain' that most climbers refer to is Catalonia, the northeast region running from the Mediterranean to the Pyrenees. Asturias, a coastal region on Spain's northern shore, is one of the lesser-known Spanish climbing spots, and an area whose quantity and quality of rock is only just starting to be whispered about.

With steep-sided, emerald-green valleys, Asturias has far more in common with similar-sounding Austria. The hills are dotted with tiny, picturesque villages, whose inhabitants wear traditional wooden clogs called *madreñas* and make cider barrels and pocket knives in the same way they have done for hundreds of years. It feels like a land lost in time.

The climbing, by comparison, is nothing like as old fashioned. While it may have been a little slower to develop than in some of the surrounding regions, modern climbing in Asturias is growing strongly, and there are plenty of challenging routes to test even the most talented of climbers. Asturias has it all: long and delicate technical slabs; short, intense boulder routes; and never-ending, overhanging tufa-fests. With over 50 crags and 3,500 routes, there is enough variety in the style of climbing to keep everyone happy.

In the centre of Asturias lies the small village of Quirós, home to some of the oldest cliffs in the region and also the Refugio del Llamo, the only climbing refuge in Asturias. The classic cliffs of Quirós stand proudly at the top of the hill, their big, blank walls inviting any climber who enjoys the more technical side of this sport to precisely place their

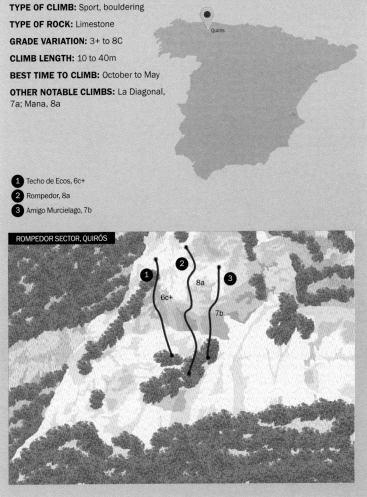

Fact File Roca Verde

TYPE OF CLIMB: Sport, bouldering

TYPE OF ROCK: Limestone

GRADE VARIATION: 3+ to 8C

CLIMB LENGTH: 10 to 40m

BEST TIME TO CLIMB: October to May

OTHER NOTABLE CLIMBS: La Diagonal, 7a; Mana, 8a

Quirós

1 Techo de Ecos, 6c+
2 Rompedor, 8a
3 Amigo Murcielago, 7b

ROMPEDOR SECTOR, QUIRÓS

feet and use brain over brawn. Challenges such as Que la Fuerza te Acompañe ('May the Force Be With You'; 7a) have stood the test of time, feeling almost as difficult today as when they were first climbed back in the 1980s.

Just around the corner, Rompedor, the first route in the area to be given the grade of 8a, tackles an unlikely looking overhang, high above one of the best views in northern Spain. Not just a route that broke through a difficulty barrier, Rompedor moved away from the traditionally vertical terrain of the slabs and walls and hinted towards where the future of climbing might go.

The number of local climbers is rather small, making the sheer number of crags and routes even more impressive. Despite the recent publication of *Roca Verde*, the first and only English-language guidebook to the climbing of the area, visitors are few and far between, and it is not uncommon to go a whole day without seeing another soul. That is, however, until the evening, when the local climbers descend on one of the area's warm and lively bars to share a locally brewed Asturian cider and a story or two about the adventures of the day.

ABOVE LEFT: James bouldering on the coast.

PREVIOUS PAGE: Caroline exploring the boulders of Teverga.

LEFT: Caroline about to begin the crux of Rompedor, with one of the best views in Spain in the background.

TOP: Walking in the tranquil village of Quirós.

ABOVE: The local cider-pouring technique, designed to put bubbles in an otherwise flat cider.

Montserrat Catalonia, Spain

Grade variation: 4+ to 9a+

BELOW: The impressive towers and faces of Montserrat.

Montserrat – not to be confused with the Caribbean island of the same name – is a small conglomerate mountain range culminating at a height of 1,236 metres, only 35 kilometres away from the city of Barcelona. It is the highest range in the Catalan lowlands, and will always impress the traveller.

Its striking conglomerate towers form a kingdom from another world, inviting climbers to dare to try one. Considered to be the cradle of the Catalan climbing scene, it has been and will continue to be the place for testing and training the best alpinists and climbers in the country. But the climbing came long after the monastery that is situated here – guardian of Catalan culture and Christian faith and the emblem of Montserrat itself. The mountains here have been of religious significance since pre-Christian times, when hermit monks built various hermitages. Today it is mostly known as the site of Santa Maria de Montserrat, a Benedictine abbey thought by some to be the location of the Holy Grail in Arthurian myth.

With such a spiritual background, and its proximity to Barcelona, Montserrat is a popular destination. The mountain range is intertwined with small paths and steps, and you could wander here for hours marvelling at the unusual rock. Pebbles from the size of fingers to televisions are shaped into towers.

In general, climbing in Montserrat is fairly precarious and requires skill, as the small, potato-like stones forming the rock threaten to spin out of the wall. Montserrat is mainly a place for slab climbing, but you can come across a few bellies and steep overhangs, though these are nearly always impossible, especially on first sight.

One of these 'impossible'-looking steep walls is Via Tarragó. It is an alien in a world of humans – a huge, 200-metre overhang in the middle of slab country. This wall had remained untouched – considered too impressive – until the Pou brothers, Eneko and Iker, aided by local friends, cleaned and worked an old aid route opened in 2001 by Montserrat local David Tarragó but not, until now, freed.

As often happens in the unfrequented routes of Montserrat, they found a lot of fragile rock, breaking in many sections, and quite a few unexpected falls occurred while cleaning the route. Finally, in early November 2013, with winter already installed on the northern side of the mountain, they made an attempt, having to dig deep to find enough strength and motivation. They made it, signing a route that puts Montserrat firmly in the 21st century.

LEFT: Eneko Pou placing gear on the lower pitches of Via Tarragó.

RIGHT: Trailing a thin rope behind the climber allows you to pull up a backpack once you reach the next belay.

NEXT PAGE: The overhanging wall of Via Tarragó is very steep, unlike the majority of Montserrat's slabs.

Fact File Montserrat

TYPE OF CLIMB: Multi-pitch bolted or trad

TYPE OF ROCK: Conglomerate

GRADE VARIATION: 4+ to 9a+

CLIMB LENGTH: Varies, but usually less than 150m

BEST TIME TO CLIMB: Spring and autumn

OTHER NOTABLE CLIMBS: Santacana, 6b; Punsola-Reniu, 6c; GAM, F6a+ A1

Montserrat

VIA TARRAGÓ, MONTSERRAT

7c+/8a
8b+
8a
8b
6b
6a+

Cova del Diablo Majorca, Spain
Grade variation: 5+ to 9a

Fifteen metres above a bright turquoise sea, hanging free from perfect orange limestone as waves crash far below your feet: this is deep-water soloing, or psicobloc, and it's hard to imagine a more exhilarating way to climb. Forget all your usual safety gear: it's just you, the rock and the water to catch you when you fall.

Deep-water soloing began on the small Spanish island of Majorca in the late 1970s, and to this day it is still one of the best places in the world to practise this crazy, cavalier sport. The combination of solid rock, steep faces and clear, deep, warm water is surprisingly hard to find, and means that every year, Majorca sees thousands of climbers flock to its shores to test their strength and nerves.

The man behind the sensation is Miquel Riera, a short, muscular, tanned Majorcan and one of the first climbers to see the possibility and potential of using the sea as a giant safety net. Riera and friends first climbed solo above the sea near the busy port of Porto Pi, and quickly realized that the island offered an almost limitless number of psicoblocs.

Psicobloc is an amalgamation of the words *psico*, the Spanish word for psycho, or psychological, and 'bloc', a shortened word that climbers use for bouldering. It's a perfect description of this style of climbing, which often includes much more intense sequences of moves than a similarly graded sport route. Since it becomes too dangerous to fall off at a height of greater than 20 metres, psicoblocs are a lot shorter than the average sport route, but a lot higher than the average bloc. Without the need to carry and place safety equipment, one has energy in reserve to invest in the moves. Yet with a potential 20-metre fall into the crashing ocean awaiting any slip, performing such intense climbing can be incredibly mentally demanding.

Driven by the thrill of climbing free and the amazing opportunity to immerse oneself in nature, Miquel Riera tirelessly and almost singlehandedly developed hundreds of psicobloc routes in Majorca. He is responsible for some of the biggest, hardest and scariest challenges around, and to this day is still developing new routes and areas along the island's seemingly never-ending coastline.

RIGHT: James dropping into the dark night while on a moonlit climbing session.

' **TO US, WE WERE SIMPLY BOULDERING** like the
Americans in Yosemite.' – Miquel Riera

'In Majorca, psicobloc arrived before sport climbing,' explained Riera in 2016. 'We were still aid climbing up mountains at the time. Then a book on Yosemite fell into our hands. Imagine: shirtless hippies, bouldering. We wanted to do that, too. In Majorca, the best place to do it was on the sea cliffs. To us, we were simply bouldering like the Americans in Yosemite.'

Deep-water soloing is an incredibly freeing form of climbing that, once experienced, is hard to forget. There is something magical about immersing oneself totally within the experience, to the extent that everything else just seems to disappear. Your first 'real' fall is a moment that will stay with you forever – not because it is terrifying, but because most likely you didn't even realize it was happening. When you commit 100 per cent to a route and fail to complete one of the movements, you'll be in the refreshing water below before you even acknowledge you are letting go.

However, don't think for one moment that psicobloc is entirely safe. It's not, and there have been many serious injuries and – more rarely – tragic fatalities. Hit the water wrong, even from a few metres high, and it can feel like hitting concrete. Sea-water enemas and bruised underarms are common injuries, but twisted knees and punctured lungs can happen to anyone entering the water slightly off-axis. It's very important to practise falling or jumping from reasonable heights to understand how to control your body in the air, as well as how to enter the water cleanly. Another good tip is to avoid using heel or toe hooks, or any other technique that places your feet high above your waist, unless absolutely

necessary. These positions are a lot more dangerous should your hands slip off or a handhold break.

For an introduction to deep-water soloing, the hidden paradise of Cala Varques is the perfect place to start. Its many small coves are rarely more than 12 metres high, and with easy access to all the routes, as well as great opportunities to spectate on the action, it's no surprise that it is also one of the busiest areas on the island.

Once you are feeling up to it, the cliff that all the other cliffs want to be is Cova del Diablo. At 20 metres tall and open to the full force of the Mediterranean, Diablo is a serious cliff and not to be taken lightly. Its premier route is Loskot and Two Smoking Barrels, a mentally demanding challenge with an 'all points off' dyno at 15 metres above the sea. First climbed by the Austrian powerhouse Klem Loskot, Smoking Barrels is named for the twin round holes that one must jump up to – or face an exhilarating plunge into the water below. The combination of immaculate rock and amazing movements is the reason why Diablo, one of the first cliffs to be developed on the island, is still considered the best deep-water solo venue in the world.

LEFT: James high up on The Weatherman, an exposed 8a+ at Cala Sa Nau.

Fact File Cova del Diablo

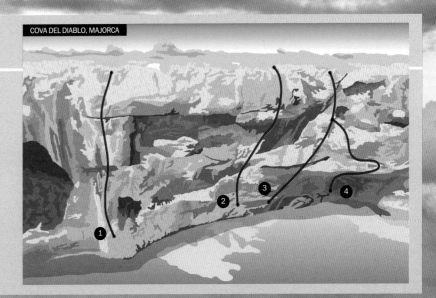

COVA DEL DIABLO, MAJORCA

TYPE OF CLIMB: Deep-water solo

TYPE OF ROCK: Limestone

GRADE VARIATION: 5+ to 9a

CLIMB LENGTH: 20m

BEST TIME TO CLIMB: May to October

OTHER NOTABLE CLIMBS: Surfing Bird, 7b; Ejector Seat, 7c+; Ronatron, 7c+

Majorca

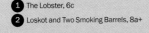

1 The Lobster, 6c

2 Loskot and Two Smoking Barrels, 8a+

3 In The Night All Cats Are Black, 8a

4 Afroman, 7b

Qualido Val di Mello, Italy
Grade variation: 6b to 8b

High in the mountains behind San Martino, a quiet, quaint village at the end of Val di Mello, Monte Qualido rises steeply from lush alpine pastures, its smooth, blank granite walls reaching over 800 metres tall. On this wall one man has carved history, opening up more routes than any other and pushing the boundaries of what was previously thought possible.

Simone Pedeferri is a curious character indeed. A climber and alpinist who has travelled the world yet never learned to drive, he is a somewhat reclusive man who runs a small, quiet bar. Pedeferri's climbing style reflects his character – drawn to the vast expanses of natural alpine granite, yet trained to physical perfection on a tiny, artificial 'bouldering wall' in his backyard.

Joy Division is one of Pedeferri's greatest achievements, and a route that has still only ever seen one repeat. It is a complicated mix of technical, physical, run-out pitches up to 8b that follows the line of an old 'aid' route up one of the steepest flanks of Qualido. To climb the twenty pitches of Joy Division in a single push requires not only great endurance, but a wide range of climbing skills to deal with the varied terrain. The route includes everything from long, delicate slabs and technical cracks to steep, powerful overhangs. It is protected by a mix of modern and ancient bolts, pitons and traditional gear, and being a high alpine granite wall, the rock itself can sometimes leave a little to be desired, demanding even more control and commitment.

'After having climbed most of the existing free lines on Monte Qualido I was looking for something to push myself and keep me entertained for the hot summer months,' explains Pedeferri. 'Joy Division is a combination of several artificial routes, with some small sections of new, independent climbing. In the end it was much harder than I expected and the first ascent demanded many weeks and months of effort.'

Monte Qualido is home to many other fantastic routes of all grades, and is a perfect location for those searching for long, top-quality routes in a quiet and infrequently visited area. Classic routes include La Spada nella Roccina ('The Sword in the Stone') and Vertical Holidays. A steep, three-hour-long hike from the valley floor means that only the truly committed come climbing here, but they are rewarded not only with amazing views and climbs, but also a silence and peace that is becoming harder and harder to find.

RIGHT: James on the first, and one of the hardest, pitches of Joy Division.

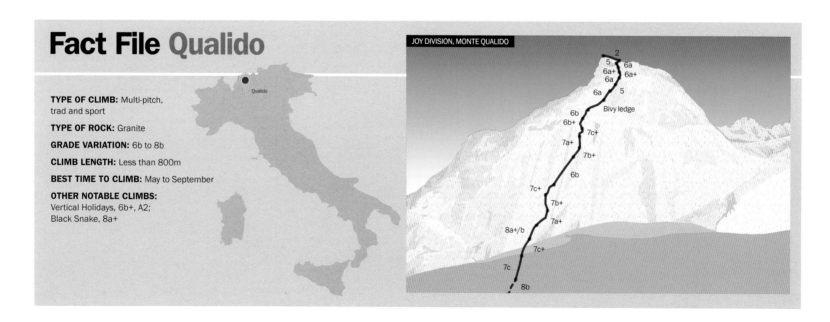

Fact File Qualido

Qualido

TYPE OF CLIMB: Multi-pitch, trad and sport

TYPE OF ROCK: Granite

GRADE VARIATION: 6b to 8b

CLIMB LENGTH: Less than 800m

BEST TIME TO CLIMB: May to September

OTHER NOTABLE CLIMBS:
Vertical Holidays, 6b+, A2;
Black Snake, 8a+

JOY DIVISION, MONTE QUALIDO

2
5
6a
6a+ 6a+
6a
6a
6a 5
6b Bivy ledge
6b+
7c+
7a+
7b+
6b
7c+
7b+
8a+/b 7a+
7c+
7c
8b

The hike up to Qualido is only possible thanks to the construction of a shepherds' path over one hundred years ago. This is not your ordinary alpine trail, but a veritable suspended staircase, at some points offering the only way up blank 30-metre-high bands of alpine granite. With a heavy pack on your back, and lungs and legs burning from the unrelenting inclination, you catch yourself marvelling at how exactly those long-ago men moved all those giant boulders perfectly into place. Feeling somehow ashamed to live in such an easy and accessible world, you mentally tip your hat to the generations that have come before, and continue slogging up the hill.

Twenty minutes from the foot of the wall, the affectionately named Hotel Qualido offers a rudimentary place for visiting climbers to sleep that, in the conditions, feels like five-star luxury. Constructed around the same time as the aforementioned staircase, Hotel Qualido is just one of a selection of ancient shepherds' huts that have recently been renovated by climbers to provide a 'comfortable' base camp. Hotel Qualido can sleep up to six people, but there are several other smaller huts dotted around the hillside where one can spend the night should the hotel be 'fully booked'. Rumour has it that slightly further up the hill, a giant shelter once existed that could house 100 goats – but all that remains now are the ancient, tumbled-down walls.

The final access to the base of the wall can be rather treacherous, especially if the grass is wet from recent rain. It is highly advised to make use of the fixed lines, as a careless unprotected slip would be catastrophic. However, do be aware that the fixed lines are often in poor condition after being left out in the elements all winter. Do yourself and all

the other climbers a favour by taking an old length of rope to replace what is already there.

Monte Qualido, and the Val di Mello in general, are fantastic places to climb, where one can find top-quality rock and quiet, tranquil surroundings – except, perhaps, during the weekend of Melloblocco, the biggest bouldering festival in the world, which takes place every May. There is every style of climbing, from bouldering to big wall, sport to trad, with plentiful cozy accommodation and authentic local cuisine. If you are looking for an all-round location for the spring and summer months, look no further.

ABOVE LEFT: The towering cliff of Qualido. The first three pitches are hidden behind the hillside.

TOP: Surveying the valley from a portaledge during one of James's early attempts on the route.
ABOVE: Climbing into the night. Headtorches light the way high up on Qualido.

Aria Sardinia, Italy
Grade variation: 8a+ EXPO

Sport climbing is the natural starting point for any novice climber. The frequent fixed bolts allow the technique of moving on rock to be developed and honed before moving on to the more complex security techniques of multi-pitch and trad climbing. The keen and ambitious climber – and those who have a true taste for rock and adrenaline – will inevitably work towards the adventure of discovering and opening new routes. But this is a long path, with much to learn along the way. There is no substitute for painstakingly learning technique and gaining the knowledge of rock, rope work and air that can only be learned via time spent on multi-pitch routes.

Multi-pitch is a fascinating element of climbing, not just because of the technical challenges it asks of the climber, but also because of what these routes can teach you about the person who has developed and freed them. You can learn so much about a climber from the way the route asks you to move, and the coolness it demands from a run-out section and all the air that is gaping below you. Nowhere is this concept better illustrated than in a remote corner of Sardinia.

Sardinia is called the 'wild island', and a forgotten piece of forest at the bottom of Punta Plumare more than does the name justice. Aria is the only line going up Punta Plumare, a wildly overhanging, 350-metre-

RIGHT: Caroline taking on one of the easier, but boldest, pitches of Aria, the fifth.

Fact File Aria

TYPE OF CLIMB: Multi-pitch

TYPE OF ROCK: Limestone

GRADE VARIATION: 8a+ EXPO

CLIMB LENGTH: 350m

BEST TIME TO CLIMB: Spring or autumn

OTHER NOTABLE CLIMBS: None – this is the only climb on the wall. There are more multi-pitches all around the island, such as on Golorize (6th grade)

Aria

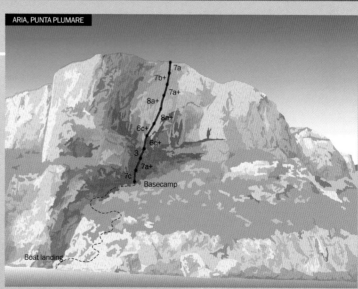

ARIA, PUNTA PLUMARE

7a
7b+
7a+
8a+
8a+
6c+
6c+
3
7a+
7c
Basecamp
Boat landing

high cliff on the east coast of Sardinia. To access the bottom of the crag, you have to take a small boat and then hike up a seemingly nonexistent path.

Camping at the foot of this wall is a relatively precarious scenario in itself, and certainly it feels incredibly remote – your company is likely to be just a handful of birds and potentially some wild pigs. Aria was opened by Pietro Dal Prà, and until recently had never been repeated.

With a grade of 8a+ maximum in 350 metres, there are harder-graded multi-pitches on the island, but the EXPO tells you that Aria will be a serious proposition. There is something about Aria that adds a special dimension to its challenge. As soon as you put a foot on the route, you realize that you have stepped into the unknown. This is the world of Pietro. The route is a sport route in the sense that it's bolted, but with no more than six bolts in each pitch, there is plenty of time to feel the air around you. The small number of bolts gives you a clue to Pietro's background as a mountain guide in his Italian home of Cortina. The years on these high and wild mountains have instilled in Pietro a deep understanding of how to manoeuvre across rock and feel comfortable with the air beneath his feet.

Pietro opened Aria from the ground up, climbing on the totally virgin rock and then using metal hooks to precariously hold on to while drilling the very few bolts. It was an incredibly bold feat that poses significant danger, and again speaks of Pietro's climbing heritage and the historic, protection-light routes of the Dolomites that were his training ground.

An intimidating first pitch of 7c wakes you up in the morning, a pitch from which Pietro himself warns you that it's 'better not to fall'. After a few easier but even bolder pitches above, you reach the meat of the route, with two 8a+ pitches on top of each other making for a testing playground, especially as the bolts remain desperately far apart. It is a hard, serious and technical line to the top.

The design of Aria's route makes this multi-pitch a spicy – and at times a somewhat scary – proposition. However, it is also an incredible place to learn, and re-learn, on the pitches of a master.

LEFT: With the sea as blue as this, it is easy to pretend you're on a beach in the Bahamas. Then you remember your partner is halfway up the hardest pitch, eight metres above the last bolt. Try to pay attention!

Rätikon The Alps
Grade variation: 5+ to 8c

The Rätikon region is a perfect example of typical Swiss Alps scenery. Long dirt roads are surrounded by fresh creeks, green fields and a lot of cows, leading you to one of the best places you could ever imagine for climbing.

Located on the borders of Austria, Switzerland and Liechtenstein, the Rätikon range was once the cradle of European multi-pitch free climbing. The smooth walls of the Kirlichspitze towers have stopped many people in their tracks, and once upon a time inspired the best local climbers to push their limits by setting new standards in alpine climbing.

The most prominent name in the history of Rätikon climbing developments is, without a doubt, Martin Scheel. Scheel pioneered many of the area's early test pieces, and is especially renowned for developing a unique style of opening new lines that not only influenced the local climbing community, but spread its way across the sport. It is a style most linked to alpine multi-pitch climbing: no prior viewing on abseil, always ground up, hooks used only for placing bolts and always climbing free between them. Those were the rules of the game that now, thirty years later, would probably make most climbers nauseous. Some may consider it an old-school approach, but others will call it ethics: either way, it is a forgotten notion for most of the modern generation of gym-raised climbers. Among the climbers that Scheel's approach influenced was an Austrian called Beat Kammerlander, a climber from Vorarlberg who has become a living legend.

Inspired by John Bachar and the activity of other climbers in Yosemite, European alpinists started treating free climbing, which is all about physical performance in the vertical, as their new philosophy. In the early 1980s, Kammerlander met Scheel. They enjoyed some sport climbing, but also exchanged ideas about what they considered important in opening new routes. Before he met Scheel, Kammerlander had been totally against bolts. His background was strongly tradition-oriented; it was all about the style. If you go to the mountains, you climb a blank-slab route, you lead and you have no equipment to drill. It's a more dangerous and more mentally testing approach than when you have a drill on your harness – if you do something stupid you can always place a bolt and go back.

However, technological development that vastly improved climbing gear opened up a new spectrum of possibilities, especially on the alpine faces that previously seemed inaccessible. After some years of chasing grades and following the single-pitch trend, Kammerlander came back to his roots, picking up where Scheel left off. After repeating some of Scheel's routes, he understood that bolts can be used simply for protection rather than aid. For him, it made perfect sense not to place bolts where it was too hard, rather placing them where it was necessary but easy, and then climbing the hard part. From this moment on, long

LEFT: The technical style of the climbing often makes the long run-outs even scarier.

PREVIOUS PAGE: Perfect vertical limestone, green hills and snowy mountains: this is the Rätikon.

Fact File Rätikon

TYPE OF CLIMB: Multi-pitch

TYPE OF ROCK: Limestone

GRADE VARIATION: 5+ to 8c

CLIMB LENGTH: Up to 400m

BEST TIME TO CLIMB: Spring to autumn

OTHER NOTABLE CLIMBS: Galadriel, 6c+; Intifada, 7a+; Lilith, 7c+

1 Antihydral
2 Silbergeier
3 Hannibal Alptraum

run-outs in the hard sections would become his style – good but serious at the same time. That decision resulted in a number of exceptional lines opening in Rätikon from 1986 to 1997, finally ending with Unendliche Geschichte (8b+), Silbergeier (8b+) and WoGü (8c), the most recognized triad. Each of them is a gem, each has a unique character and each was way ahead of its time. It's important to remember that, even if most routes are bolted, it doesn't mean that they are an easy task. There are often very few bolts, and the technical style of the climbing often makes the long run-outs even scarier.

Beat Kammerlander was an innovator and a visionary. He was always searching for something new that would push the sport of climbing, especially when it came to opening new routes. But Rätikon is not just about hard and intimidating routes; everyone will find their own challenge on these smooth walls. Routes such as Intifada, Lillith, New Age and Galadriel, to mention just a few, belong to a selection of the best multi-pitches in the Alps. It is truly hard to beat the beauty of their pitches and rock.

Kammerlander's style, mixed with Rätikon's history and idyllic setting, is the precise combination that defines the essence of this vastly popular and exciting climbing destination.

RIGHT: The peaks of the Rätikon jut out of the land like the spine of some primordial beast.

Ticino Switzerland
Grade variation: 3+ to 8C

In November 2000, Swiss bouldering legend Fred Nicole made the first ascent of Dreamtime, a long-term project of his on one of the biggest boulders in Cresciano, in Ticino, Switzerland. Not only was Dreamtime the world's first 8C boulder, it also put Swiss bouldering on the international climbing map, setting it on a path to becoming one of the most famous bouldering locations in the world.

The southern Swiss, Italian-speaking canton of Ticino is the youngest part of modern Switzerland, having been taken from Italy sometime in the 15th century. Today, over 350,000 people live in Ticino and, apart from being home to Switzerland's third-largest financial centre, Lugano, it is also one of the main trade areas for the outdoor tourism industry in Europe.

Climbers have been exploring Ticino's fantastic hills and mountains for decades before the first boulderer ever lay down his crash pad, but it is bouldering that has made Ticino world famous. The compact, fine-grained granite is pure pleasure to climb upon, and Mother Nature has seen fit to grace us with hundreds of thousands of incredible boulders, most of which still lie undiscovered in the forest, waiting for the first climber to mark their path.

Without doubt, Cresciano is the most famous of the Ticino bouldering areas, as well as being one of its oldest. These days, however, there are many other sectors that can compete with Cresciano for both quantity and quality, arguably with even better rock. Brione is one such area. Tucked away in a high alpine valley, far up beyond one of the highest dams in Europe, Brione is a microcosm of Switzerland in all its perfect glory. Fat, happy cows chew grass in green pastures, with dark forests fading into pointy, snow-covered mountains far behind. Bouldering up in Brione is simply magnificent, and guaranteed to put a smile on your face whatever the grade.

Brione's list of five-star boulders goes on and on, but its crowning glory has to be Vecchio Leone ('Old Lion'). At 8B it is also one of Brione's hardest blocs, but its majesty comes mainly from its position and its visual beauty. Vecchio Leone sits all alone on an enormous boulder high up in the woods. A line of perfect holds leads up a tall, gently overhanging

OPPOSITE: James attempting to figure out the technical sequence on Village Idiot, Sonlerto.

Fact File Ticino

TYPE OF CLIMB: Boulder

TYPE OF ROCK: Granite

GRADE VARIATION: 3+ to 8C

CLIMB LENGTH: 2 to 10m

BEST TIME TO CLIMB: October to April

OTHER NOTABLE CLIMBS:
Black Mirror, 6C; Molunk, 7C; Amber, 8B

Brione

VECCHIO LEONE, BRIONE

wall of splendid, fine-grained granite. Towards the top of the wall, the hardest move takes the aspiring climber past a hold formed from a single, giant quartz crystal. One final 'heartbreaker' move lands you in a narrow, awkward slot, from where large holds lead easily to the top, and victory.

The most beautiful things often come with their own issues, and Brione is no exception. Long before climbers first began to explore this magical place, Brione was a tiny farming village, accessible only by a steep hiking track. Today, the village is mostly filled with second homes, but nonetheless, Brione's regular occupants became understandably vexed with the hundreds of newcomers descending on their tranquil houses and sometimes not even respecting the boundaries of their gardens. A delicate equilibrium now exists, where climbers visit only in the winter months when the village is mostly empty.

Should you ever find yourself high up in that beautiful place, enjoy all the wonders it can offer you and climb to your heart's content – but remember to spare a thought for the people who call it home.

OPPOSITE: James crimping hard on The Great Shark Hunt, Chironico.

BELOW: One of the best boulders in Switzerland, Vecchio Leone.

Zillertal Tyrol, Austria
Grade variation: 3+ to 8B+; 3+ to 9a+

There are few places in Europe that can compete with Austria for raw, natural beauty. Wide, flat-bottomed valleys are dotted with picturesque villages and flanked on either side by steep, forest-covered mountains. The clanging bells of dairy cows out to pasture are ever present, forgotten only when replaced with the noise of thundering alpine waterfalls crashing down into deep, sheer-sided gorges.

Austria has a long and rich history of mountain climbing, but until recent years was a little behind the pack when it came to pure sport rock climbing. It's funny how fashion and focus change, and sometimes all it takes is a little spark to start a fire. Nowadays the Austrian rock-climbing scene is ablaze with some of the best climbers in the world, in all disciplines from big wall to bouldering. Austria is leading the way in showing just how powerful at sports a small country can be with the right direction and motivation.

The home of Austrian climbing is the small city of Innsbruck, host of the Winter Olympics in both 1964 and 1976. Despite the undeniable success of Austrian climbers, Innsbruck's main sporting focus is on skiing and football, and Innsbruck's climbing wall is tucked away in a corner of FC Wacker's giant stadium. The structure is dated and overcrowded, yet is has been the meeting point for the Tyrolean climbing community as well as the training ground for some of the best competition climbers in the world.

Surrounded by mountains, Innsbruck has many good climbing spots in close proximity to the city, but for truly world-class climbing one has to travel a little further afield. Located just past the ski resort of Mayrhofen, the alpine valley of the Zillertal has it all. Bouldering, sport, trad, multi-pitch, alpine … the list goes on. The rock in the Zillertal can vary wildly in both quality and form, from close-grained, water-polished granite in the riverbeds to exfoliating gneiss high up on the mountain ridges. Without a doubt, the most popular climbing spots are the large 'boulders' of Ewige Jagdgründe. Whilst technically boulders, these giant blocks of granite fell down from the mountain top millennia ago and are now covered by some of Austria's best sport routes, some of them more than 20 metres long.

Sport climbing in the Zillertal is very different to the more traditional styles on the cliffs of France or Spain. Generally speaking the routes tend to have far harder movements, but also far better rest, and are

ABOVE: James climbing The Source, perhaps the finest masterpiece of Gerhard Hörhager.

OPPOSITE: Love 2.1 – one of the routes chipped by a previous generation and now restored to its former glory.

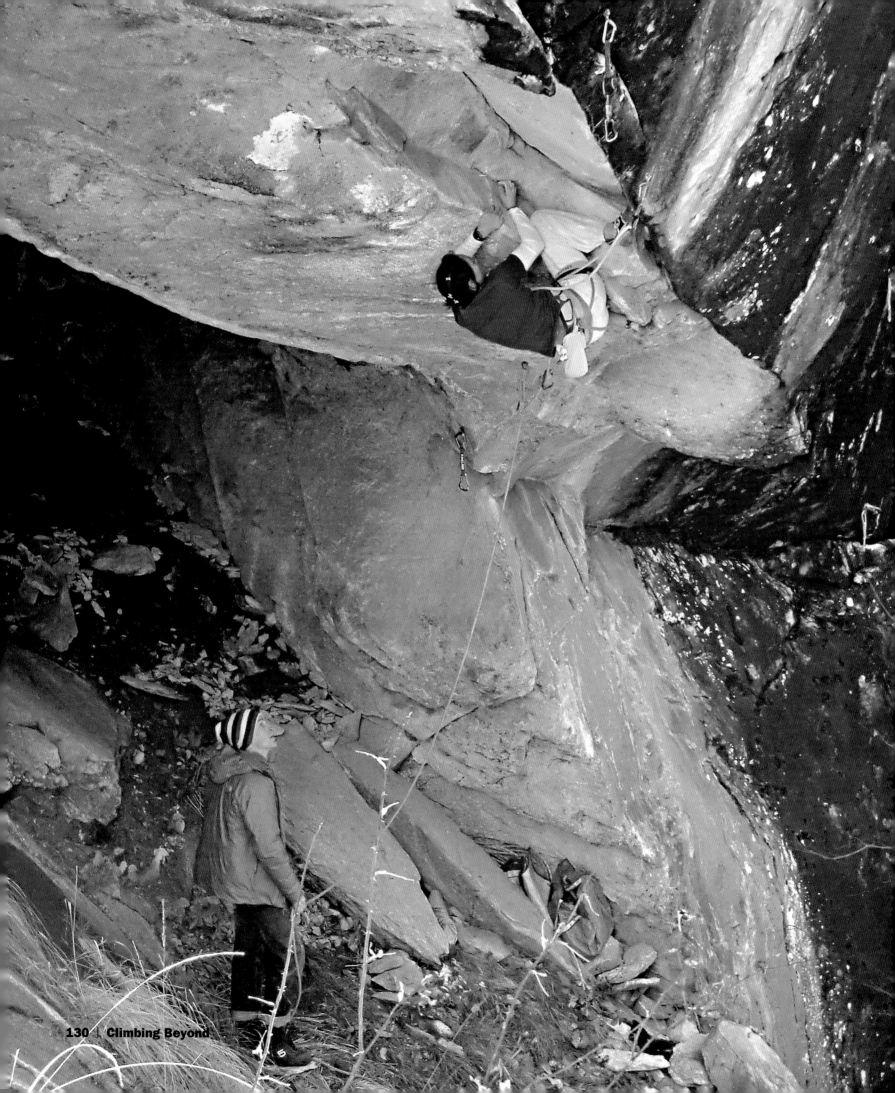

much better suited to boulderers than endurance route climbers. There is perhaps no better example of this than Gracelands, a short 8b route that is better described as a 7C+ boulder with a rope.

Gracelands was first climbed way back in 1986 by Gerhard Hörhager, one of the first of Austria's new generation of climbers. Gerhard was training for sport climbing competitions at the time, but found that his power-based style, honed on the granite of the Zillertal, was a poor match for the long, endurance style of the competitions. He originally graded Gracelands 7c+, as that was the maximum grade he had climbed on other rocks. However, when some of the shining stars of the competition world came to visit and no one could climb the route, people started to wonder if it might not be a bit harder.

In an effort to simulate the routes of the competitions, Gerhard and some of the other strong Austrian climbers decided to manufacture artificial holds on some of the blank, impossible-looking faces. Chipping was common practice in the 1980s and 1990s, yet nowadays it is frowned upon. In twenty years our vision of climbing and our understanding of the limits has completely flipped. Good-quality rock is hard and rare, and naturally climbable routes are held in much higher regard.

Nowadays the Zillertal enjoys a thriving local climbing scene, with regular visitors from all around the world. Gerhard is still climbing just as hard as ever, and regularly develops new crags and routes. He even repaired some of the old chipped routes to their natural states, and subsequently re-climbed them to conquer some of the area's hardest test pieces. Gerhard recently opened a small bed and breakfast, the Diggl Climbers and Freeride Farm, at his family home in the village of Ginzling, from where he runs guided tours of the best climbing, skiing and mountain biking in the area. With a climbing wall, sauna and plunge pool built into some of the old cow sheds, it's a place you might never want to leave.

❝ ... THE ZILLERTAL HAS IT ALL.

Bouldering, sport, trad, multi-pitch, alpine ... the list goes on.'

Fact File Zillertal

TYPE OF CLIMB: Bouldering, sport, multi-pitch

TYPE OF ROCK: Granite

GRADE VARIATION: 3+ to 8B+; 3+ to 9a

CLIMB LENGTH: 2 to 200m

BEST TIME TO CLIMB: Spring to autumn

OTHER NOTABLE CLIMBS: Sechsplosion, 6c; Sagaro, 8a+

Zillertal

1 No U Turn, 6b+
2 Muttertag, 7b+
3 Graceland, 8b
4 The Meatcheesecrack, 7c
5 Das letzte Einhorn, 6b+
6 Der Weg durch das Puff, 6b

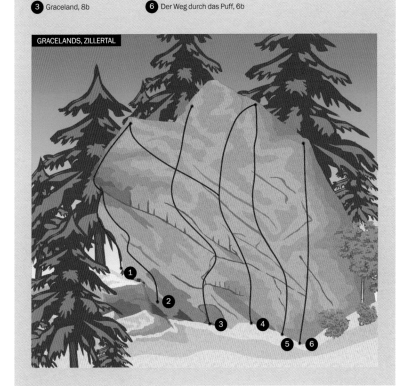

GRACELANDS, ZILLERTAL

LEFT: Sprungbrettl at the Schwarze Wand is more like wrestling than climbing. An excellent upside-down adventure.

The Elbe Valley
Decín, Czech Republic

Grade variation: IV+ to XI

There are a few locations in this world that strike fear into the hearts of all climbers, and the rocks of the Czech Republic are one such place. Famed for its impressive sandstone towers, with their own set of strict climbing regulations, the Czech Republic offers a truly rare experience.

Reputations of this sort are usually based in some sort of truth, but keep an open mind and you might be pleasantly surprised. In walking their own path, the adventurous travelling climber can discover all the wonder and magic that this world has to offer. And this can certainly be true here.

Overlooking the River Elbe and surrounded by thick pine forests, the secluded crags of Dolní Žleb are undoubtedly Czech. Rustic pubs that seem to be stuck in time serve beer by the litre, and locals slap you on the back and break into big grins when they see you struggle to lift up your glass.

It's hard to say exactly when climbing began in Dolní Žleb, but it's safe to say that native climbers have been exploring these sandstone outcrops for generations. Unlike the extreme ethics of the nearby Adršpach, which relies on a curious collection of knotted slings for safety equipment, Dolní Žleb is slightly less severe and the majority of the routes are completely protected by oversized iron ringbolts. This is sport climbing, Czech style – it's safe, as long as you choose your place to fall off wisely.

The decision to space these bolts so far apart is based on several factors, but is mainly the result of how the routes have been created in the first place. All of the rock climbs at Dolní Žleb have been bolted from the ground up – a difficult, time-consuming process rarely used in the modern sport-climbing world. This is just one of the requirements of bolting in the Czech Republic, the powers that be believing that it will

BELOW: Stunning routes and stunning locations are abundant.

help preserve the ever-diminishing quantity of unclimbed rock for future generations. In addition, bolts must be drilled by hand rather than with the usual accompaniment of an electric hammer drill. Without even going into the logistical complications of getting yourself into position, a single hole can take up to 30 exhausting minutes to drill, tapping and turning away at the hand chisel while praying that your precariously placed skyhooks don't part company with the rock. In simple terms, bolting routes here is slow, exhausting and scary, and as such the climbs tend towards using as few bolts as possible.

Despite these unusual climbing traits, Dolní Žleb is an incredible place to climb, predominantly because the rock is simply magnificent. The sandstone cliffs are an extraordinary combination of all things great about climbing. The holds are sculpted and smooth, the rock is grippy but not aggressive, and the moves flow effortlessly yet still demand focus and concentration.

Once in full understanding of the conditions and regulations for climbing in this area, Dolní Žleb makes an incredible 'off the beaten track' destination for any sport climber. And for those climbers who consider a sense of risk as part of the reward, there really are few places better.

RIGHT: Just make sure you are comfortable with spaced bolting, as some of the routes are rather run-out.

PREVIOUS PAGE: The Elbe Valley in the Czech Republic is one of Europe's best-kept climbing secrets.

RIGHT: Jeptiška, first ascended in 1906, was one of the first towers to be climbed in the Elbe Valley.

Fact File The Elbe Valley

TYPE OF CLIMB: Adventure, sport

TYPE OF ROCK: Sandstone

GRADE VARIATION: IV+ to XI

CLIMB LENGTH: 10 to 30m

BEST TIME TO CLIMB: Spring and autumn

OTHER NOTABLE CLIMBS:
Amore Mio, 6b;
Hop Nebo Trop, 7b+

Dolní Žleb

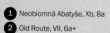 Neoblomná Abatyše, Xb, 8a

 Old Route, VII, 6a+

JEPTIŠKA, THE ELBE VALLEY

Prohodna Cave Karlukovo, Bulgaria
Grade variation: 5+ to 9a

The Balkan Peninsula is dominated by the Balkan Mountains, which cut like a knife through the region and form the watershed between Greece and the Black Sea. Running through Bulgaria for 560 kilometres from Serbia to the Black Sea coast, they have been a major player in the nation's long and colourful history. The stunning views from the Shipka Pass and its memorial to those who died for the liberation of Bulgaria – and the 1981 remnant of communism at Buzludzha, which has since fallen into disuse – are both important symbols of Bulgaria's history and are found in the midst of the mountains.

To the south, Bulgaria borders Greece; to the east is the Black Sea; north sits the powerful Danube before the border with Romania; and to the west it is bordered by Macedonia and Serbia. The region and its surrounding countries are the ultimate road-trip destination. Stunning scenery, quiet towns and countries with comparatively small populations make for a fascinating adventure. But it's the mountains and their huge expanse that most distinguish these varied countries.

Bulgaria is certainly a country for the great outdoors, no matter where you come from. There are many alpine-style regions, along with lakes, rivers, caves and most noticeably trees, as far as the eye can see. The capital, Sofia, is overlooked by a ski resort, and there is plenty of deep-water soloing, bouldering, traditional climbing, multi-pitch sport climbing and caving. Rila, the region's highest peak at 2,925 metres, sits proudly to the south of Sofia and provides super granite bouldering in the summer and skiing in winter. The bouldering is undocumented, remaining a voyage of discovery on which any climber may embark.

Bulgaria is dominated by limestone scenery, in which karst and caves abound. It is famous for its cave formations, and one of the most stunning is Devetashka Cave, with its seven windows to the sky. Sadly there is no climbing here, as inside live 12 species of protected amphibians, 82 bird species, 34 species of mammals and 15 species of bats. There are usually around 30,000 bats in the cave.

For cave climbing in Bulgaria there really is only one place to go. Prohodna Cave, meaning Passage Cave, is located near the village of Karlukovo and is famous for its perfectly formed windows into the outside world. The very aptly named 'Eyes of God', or Oknata, dominate the centre of the cave's tube-like formation. At each end of the 262-metre-long tube, the gaping arches are between 35 and 45 metres high. Climbing exists throughout the whole cave, however, not just at the entrances. The windows provide enough light for climbing and the cave provides a cool and comfortable atmosphere when the outside summer temperature soars.

In 2014, the Petzl RocTrip came to town and showed off Prohodna in all its glory. The RocTrips are a yearly event focused on the discovery and development of incredible new climbing areas. The best climbers and equippers from all around the world are invited for one week of intense climbing and bolting, and they are often the spark that lights the fire for future local development. And so it was in Bulgaria. The presence and motivation of visiting superstars such as Dani Andrada was the impetus that led to Bulgaria's first 9a. Bolted way back in 2007 by Ivailo Radkov-Fazata and Boiko Lalov, the 50-metre line finishes through one of the eyes after 50 metres of steep and relentless climbing. Radkov-Fazata made the first ascent of his dream project in August 2015 and laid down the challenge for generations to come.

Prohodna has everything, from routes for beginners to some of the most futuristic lines around. Tufas, huecos, jugs, crimps and blobs are everywhere, making every route varied and interesting. A classic example of this is the aptly named 7a, Oh Wow. The route is 25 metres of pure climbing pleasure, as it weaves an intricate path via some amazing dinner-plate-sized flakes up a steadily steepening wall. When things really start to kick in, a tufa arrives and, with an ever-steepening angle, you reach the sanctuary of a large hueco and the belay is clipped.

It's safe to say that the development of climbing in Bulgaria will continue to flourish, not only in the many magnificent caves, but all around the country. The local climbers know what they have and how to make the most of it. The fire is burning now, and nobody can put it out.

OPOOSITE: In Prohodna Cave, one can find everything – slabs, walls, overhangs, crimps, holes and tufas.
NEXT PAGE: The sheer scale of Prohodna Cave has to be seen (or climbed) to be believed.

Fact File Prohodna Cave

TYPE OF CLIMB: Sport

TYPE OF ROCK: Limestone

GRADE VARIATION: 5+ to 9a

CLIMB LENGTH: 12 to 40m

BEST TIME TO CLIMB: Spring and autumn

OTHER NOTABLE CLIMBS: Triagalnikat, 7b+;
Napred I Nagore, 9a

Prohodna Cave

1. Oh Wow, 7a
2. Severozapad, 7a+
3. Sever, 7b+
4. Mlechen Pat, 7b
5. Project
6. Triagalnikat, 7b+

PROHODNA CAVE, KARLUKOVO

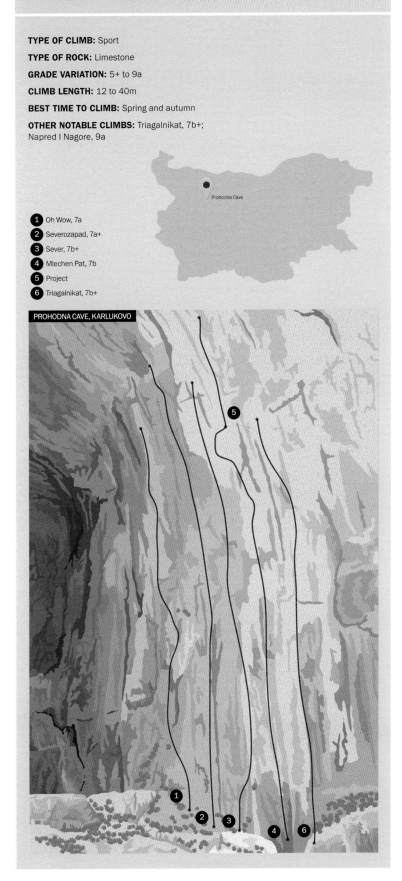

LEFT: The 'eyes' in the roof of the cave allow light to enter and air to circulate.

TOP: It is possible to climb in the cave even during the hot summer months.
ABOVE: The steep climbing here is extremely physical.

Metéora Kalabaka, Greece
Grade variation: 3+ to 8b+

Why do humans climb? These days we refer to sport, the challenge of it, overcoming your fears ... but what if it were part of your world, what if you were climbing to provide your goats with a better pasture, or to escape invaders? Necessity makes you stronger, and in Metéora it would seem that, five centuries ago, men were climbing up to the fifth grade as part of their everyday lives.

Metéora is most well known for its Orthodox monasteries, perched atop giant conglomerate towers in the centre of mainland Greece. There is something truly special in this landscape, with its dark-green oaks, its pomegranate trees and the ancient village of Metéora, nowadays full of restaurants and hostels.

In the modern climbing world, Metéora has become known as a unique adventure-climbing location. You pass a turn in the road, and suddenly you are in a field of towers 150 metres high, some capped by monasteries. Here are the Metéora rocks, described as having 'fallen from the sky' – they are an incredible sight. And indeed, their presence

is surprising. When the Orthodox monks arrived to build the first monastery around 1340, they were actually attempting to escape their enemies rather than trying to 'get closer to the sky'. They turned to the village and those who knew the secrets of the Metéora – the villagers who would help them reach the unreachable through hidden faults of the rock. The locals had been climbing for a long time already, perhaps to escape invaders or maybe for the thrill of climbing as we know it today. We will never know, but today their legacy holds true, and you can find several traces of ancient human presence in places only accessible while properly climbing.

In the 1950s, shepherds would climb to access untouched pastures on top of the towers, then drop a rope and haul their goats up. They would leave them up there, collecting them back at the end of the season. In the village of Kastraky, it is known that two shepherds died in the process.

In Metéora, you will have to choose between the 'modern' routes,

LEFT: Almost there ... The Spindle is one of the thinnest towers at Metéora.

bolted normally, and the old routes, referred to as 'classics'. The Spindle tower is a 50-metre spine of rock. On first sight it seems incredibly thin, and you wonder how solid the rock can be. The first challenge is to actually spot the start of the route. There are at least five metres without anything that could be called a bolt, nor is there any natural protection. At this stage you would be brave enough to continue with only a sling around a bigger pebble, but you can't find even that consolation. Search some more, and you may be lucky enough to spot a very strange ring attached to a metal nail. That's it – you're on the right path. And that is all you'll have for protection. As fragile as the cement may seem, even pebbles more than half out don't seem to move. Where your senses tell you to be careful, your brain has to convince them otherwise. It is solid, but it is essential to stick to the route or you will soon realize that the pebbles are not all that settled in some places. Once you feel confident on the starting pitch, you will have received the Spindle's stern warning, and it is a fairly easy run up to the next pitch to the summit. It's an extremely exposed climb – though fairly accessible technique-wise, you are fully aware that you are in the air.

If your hands and feet cry for mercy after days of climbing, you could aim instead to reach the top of one of the old monasteries, now deserted and falling to pieces. There were once 24 Orthodox monasteries, but today only six remain, and of these only three are inhabited. Be careful at the very top, while climbing over the ramshackle stone walls. You are now on top of the world, just like the monks were so long ago. You will find the well still full of water and discover the old rooms, the haulage system to bring food up from the bottom and the entrance to this very special place. It is nearly time to go down, but take a few more minutes to write in the route book that lies in the middle of the monastery, protected in a metal case and waiting for climbers to find it.

Metéora was the first place that people climbed in Greece, long before they started to develop the modern limestone crags nearby. And Metéora is the place to which they return, when they want a little bit of something 'more'. Is it the beauty of the place that makes it so special, or the spiritual influence of the monasteries? Or perhaps just the rock itself, and the spirit in which the routes have been opened. There is something really different here, something special. Something that tells you: just go.

LEFT: Caroline climbing Diagonian Devil, one of the rare overhanging sport routes at Metéora.

Fact File Metéora

TYPE OF CLIMB: Adventure, sport, multi-pitch

TYPE OF ROCK: Conglomerate

GRADE VARIATION: 3+ to 8b+

CLIMB LENGTH: 10 to 120m

BEST TIME TO CLIMB: September to April

OTHER NOTABLE CLIMBS: Hammer und Sichel, 6b+; Orchidea, 7b+

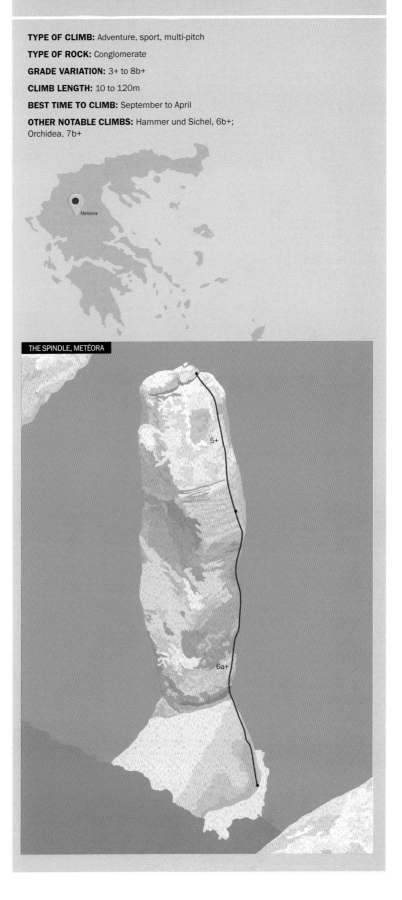

THE SPINDLE, METÉORA

5+

6a+

Kaynaklar Izmir, Turkey
Grade variation: 4+ to 8b+

LEFT: Caroline enjoying one of Kaynaklar's many amazing tufas.

Fact File Kaynaklar

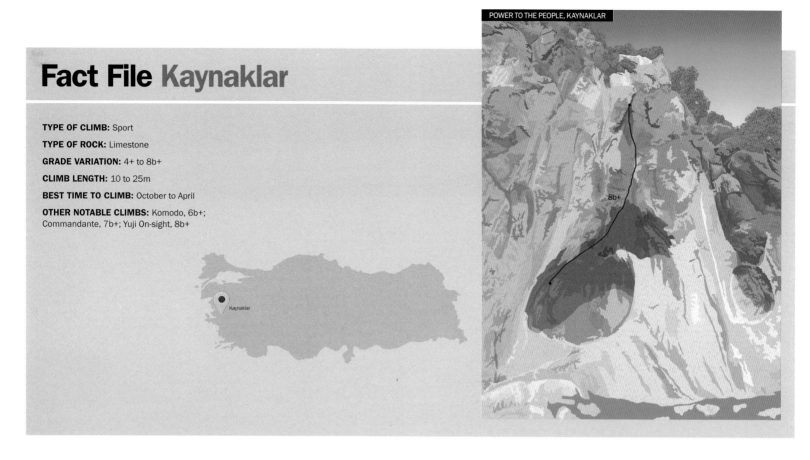

POWER TO THE PEOPLE, KAYNAKLAR

8b+

TYPE OF CLIMB: Sport

TYPE OF ROCK: Limestone

GRADE VARIATION: 4+ to 8b+

CLIMB LENGTH: 10 to 25m

BEST TIME TO CLIMB: October to April

OTHER NOTABLE CLIMBS: Komodo, 6b+;
Commandante, 7b+; Yuji On-sight, 8b+

Kaynaklar

Climbers from all over the world come every year to Antalya, Turkey's most infamous climbing paradise. They come to put their hands on the beautiful tufa routes, and also for a taste of local specialities such as *gözleme* (pancakes) and *bazlama* (griddled flatbread). However, an alternative to this Turkish climbing mecca can be found near Izmir, to the northwest of Turkey, for an arguably much more authentic experience.

On Saturday mornings, the small town of Kaynaklar is buzzing. Its local market is packed full of fresh fruits, homemade olives, chillies, preserved vegetables, honey and bread. The market is just past the centre of town, which is beautifully dominated by a towering, 800-year-old tree. Just 400 metres from this spot is a vast camping and picnic area – the resting ground for climbers who are planning routes and recovering from the overhanging cliffs just beyond the olive trees.

The cliffs at Kaynaklar were developed some 20 years ago, and now have over 200 routes from 4+ onwards. The Kaynaklar cliffs are not as vast as they are at Turkey's other climbing hot spot, Antalya, and the routes are significantly shorter, at just 15 metres on average, but there is still plenty of fun to be had on these tufas.

One of the most striking routes, Power To The People, is an 8b+ and one of the hardest routes of the crag. Starting on the edge of a cave, it has a direct line between tufa blobs in the roof to a dynamic 'heartbreaker' of a last move – a very physical challenge indeed. There is no doubt about it, these are very hard movements – but that is the fun of Kaynaklar. The route was originally bolted by Zorbey Aktuyun, an active bolter and one of Turkey's climbing sensations. Aktuyun has begun to make a name for himself – like many of the region's hardest climbing challenges, until very recently this route had only been climbed by him.

Watching Aktuyun expertly navigate this cliff, you soon realize how 'lonely' he is at this elite level in this part of the world, where climbing is still a relatively young sport. Repetitions of routes above 8a in Kaynaklar are still unusual events.

Aktuyun is always happy to see other climbers repeat his routes, as this is his chance to get feedback on their quality and difficulty – which often leads to opening new routes and thinking about climbing in new ways. Aktuyun's world is one of discovery, and not having the footsteps of a previous generation in which to follow has allowed him to create his own definitive technique, built out of 'stubbornness and weirdness,' as he himself describes. 'When I was 17, I went to Bafa, further north on the coast, for months. There are boulders of granite there, and nowadays Bafa has acquired a climbing reputation. But at that time, nobody in Turkey knew what bouldering was, nobody understood even the bouldering grades. There, I learned my technique alone, my fingers got strong, and when I came back to routes, I was good.'

It is one thing to learn climbing in a super-modern climbing gym, following your elders, listening to your trainer and reaching unbelievable levels of fitness. It all demands a tremendous amount of discipline and toughness. However, it is another thing altogether to learn alone, train alone, rise alone. It is something truly inspiring, and the cliffs at Kaynaklar are the perfect place in which to appreciate it.

RIGHT: Power To The People
involves a succession of beautiful,
powerful movements.

Africa

The Ennedi Desert Chad
Grade variation: E1 to E7

A great explorer has the right mix of adventure, dreams and the ability to take a risk. Just like the epic explorers from centuries ago, Mark Synnott is not afraid to step off the beaten track in search of his dreams and, more often than not, find something extraordinary. After graduating from college in 1993, Synnott, already a motivated climber, had no idea where life would take him. After spending 39 days living on the side of a 1,550-metre rock face whilst attempting the first ascent of the Polar Sun Spire on Baffin Island in northeastern Canada, Synnott knew little more about what his future might hold – only that it would be anything other than ordinary. Mark has visited and established new climbs in places as extreme and exotic as Patagonia and the Pitcairn Islands, yet it is the Ennedi Desert in northeastern Chad that he considers to be his greatest discovery.

The Ennedi Desert lies over 1,000 kilometres from the country's capital, N'Djamena. Chad, sometimes referred to as 'the dead heart of Africa', is not one of the first places one thinks of for a climbing trip.

Yet after discovering vast fields of rock via satellite imagery, Synnott decided it was 'probably worth a look', and put together the first-ever climbing expedition to the Ennedi in November 2010. The heart of the Ennedi is reached only by driving through the sands – 800 kilometres of sands, to be precise. There are no roads out there; instead one simply follows a GPS bearing and, if you are lucky, the tyre tracks of vehicles that have passed before.

There is little vegetation in this extreme heat, and as you travel further away from the capital, little quickly fades to nothing. It is only

LEFT: The Arch of Bishekele, one of James's proudest first ascents.

after four days' driving from N'Djamena that a faint blur on the horizon forms into cliff bands that, as you draw closer, arrange themselves into isolated domes and finally become complex arrangements of towers and arches. The incredible sight of jagged rocks breaking the flat of the desert is a calling card to any eager-eyed climber. Their form and shapes are both intriguing and intimidating – structures that hint at what it might be possible to achieve in the days to come.

'We were giddy with excitement. We had never seen a set of rocks like these. New, unclimbed rocks with seemingly endless possibilities,' recalls Synnott, who laid claim to the first climb of the formations with James Pearson. 'Every day we left camp in search of the perfect line. If we found something worthy, we would camp there for as long as it took; if not, we would keep on searching. Three-star lines became a formality, so much so that they also became monotonous – amazingly, we were looking for something even better.'

On a ten-day tour of the Ennedi, Pearson and Synnott, along with teammate Alex Honnold, established four major lines: The Citadel, The Wine Bottle, The Roof Crack and The Arch, each on a stunning, unique rock formation, but there is infinitely more rock to develop. They dealt with extreme heat, unrelenting sickness and even attacks from bandits, yet all three agree that their experience in the Ennedi has made memories to last a lifetime.

Chad, one of the newest and most remote areas to be explored by climbers in recent years, offers adventurous climbers a dream experience. As Pearson describes, 'In a world where everything seems to have been discovered, it's rare to find your own place, but there, atop those magnificent towers, you are at peace.'

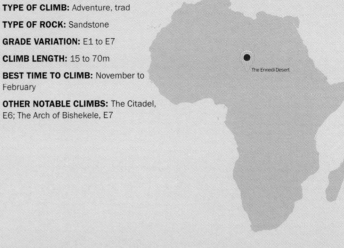

Fact File The Ennedi Desert

TYPE OF CLIMB: Adventure, trad

TYPE OF ROCK: Sandstone

GRADE VARIATION: E1 to E7

CLIMB LENGTH: 15 to 70m

BEST TIME TO CLIMB: November to February

OTHER NOTABLE CLIMBS: The Citadel, E6; The Arch of Bishekele, E7

The Ennedi Desert

THE WINE BOTTLE, THE ENNEDI DESERT

E7

E5

LEFT: James and Mark on the first belay of The Wine Bottle, with their camp and jeep down below.

Tafraout <small>Morocco</small>
Grade variation: 4+ to 8A; 5+ to 8b; VS to E8

Coming to Morocco in January, especially if you reside in colder climates, is as easy a decision for the avid climber as clapping your hands. Its glorious heat and incredible scenery are like a different world. There are some destinations that a climber chooses for the rock, for the famous routes or for the climbing community that they will encounter there – other destinations are for all the rest.

In Tafraout, there is no proper topo, no exhaustive list of routes or boulders. There are a few descriptions recorded – a couple of pages' worth of routes, a vague description of access – but not much and certainly not extensive. But the rock is there. Everywhere.

Tafraout is a tiny town in Tiznit province, almost a village, set in a niche between hills in a desert of rock. From the terraced roofs and cafés serving the freshest of orange juice, you can turn on your heels and see a beautiful line of hills filled with round boulders in every direction. In the intense heat, it is best to set off early into the warm air and the mineral kingdom.

The rock is rough at first touch, a big, grainy granite. Low in the valley, it's even rougher but strangely, sometimes, tender as well – it crumbles at the lightest of touches. 100 metres higher, on top of every little hill, the wind leaves only the more solid grains in place, and that is where the better rock lies.

With no printed topo available, it is possible to come back to what climbing should be: a line of features that catch your eye, attract you and inspire you to answer their call. Maybe it will work, maybe it won't: potentially the rock will be too hard, offer no possible holds or protection ... but as with all great climbing spots, you will only know by putting your hands on the rock. This is simple climbing; real climbing.

There is sand on the plains, only a few palm trees and spiky bushes for vegetation and, where the hill starts, boulders. Take a few crash pads, but not so many as not to be able to walk a lot, and you can play for a full day. The town is only five minutes away, but other than the possibility of a couple of curious children coming to watch, it offers a solitude like few other places in the world. You turn a corner and there they are, the painted blue rocks that Tafraout is famous for. The scenery almost looks Photoshopped, but it's definitely real, albeit enhanced.

RIGHT: Some of the painted boulders of Jean Veran.
PREVIOUS PAGE: Tafraout is a land of rock.

Fact File Tafraout

AMALU WALL, TAFRAOUT

TYPE OF CLIMB: Bouldering, sport, trad, multi-pitch

TYPE OF ROCK: Granite

GRADE VARIATION: 4+ to 8A; 5+ to 8b; VS to E8

CLIMB LENGTH: 2 to 30m

BEST TIME TO CLIMB: December to March

OTHER NOTABLE CLIMBS: El Tocho, 8a+/b

Tafraout

1 Living Like Shadows, 7a

2 Ninja Bereber, 7b

3 Morocco Airlines, 7c

Back in the 1980s, a Belgian artist called Jean Veran and his team used eighteen tonnes of paint to colour the boulders.

Higher up the hills lie the bigger boulders. If you are lucky with the holds, a trad rack will sometimes allow you to reach a little piece of virgin land, the summit of a hill perhaps never touched by man. The rock is still free there, unclimbed. The routes wait for an adventurous climber to reveal them, and the views beg for it to be achieved. From this point you can spot the small, white town of Tafraout, and on the far horizon lies the Atlas mountain chain, looking like the beginning of the world. As Talo Martin says, 'Tafraout is a wonderful, magical place, full of colourful rocks and even more colourful people.' The top of that hill is where you'll celebrate this, along with your decision to travel to a tiny town in the middle of the Moroccan desert.

BELOW: Caroline making the first ascent of an easy boulder in the Garden of Eden.

OPPOSITE, TOP: Climbing new problems often starts with cleaning the rock.
OPPOSITE, CENTRE: Once clean, the holds can be used and the rock becomes a route.
OPPOSITE, BOTTOM: Just another new problem in Tafraout.

The Cederberg South Africa
Grade variation: 5 to 8C; 6a to 8b+; VS to E9

For climbers, South Africa can be a big adventure or a small one. It is all about the type of climber that you want to be for the time that you will have there.

In Europe, much of the rock has already been climbed, topographed and certainly talked about. Climbers from the 1960s onwards invented climbing in Europe. They explored and defined its rules and have signed the big routes that novice climbers can only dream of. For some climbers today, it can feel as if you have come too late to the party.

However, without the routes already developed, the new horizons now opening on the climbing scene would not be possible. And for that, we definitely have it easier. We can be the kids of a generation that offered us climbing and gave us the keys to the most exciting playground in the world.

In the southern hemisphere, however, there is still more rock waiting to be climbed. Even if, as elsewhere, there is a long history of alpinism and established climbing groups, there are still so many new discoveries to be made.

BELOW: There are few paved roads in Rocklands, just miles and miles of dirt tracks.

OPPOSITE: Looking for new lines, high up in the Cederberg.

Fred Nicole, Tod Skinner and Scott Milton opened a lot of the vast boulder field that is now Rocklands, which sits in the Cederberg mountains just three hours north of Cape Town. This beautiful setting has an abundance of rock – a true playground for any climber to try and climb a lifetime of boulders – and even the possibility to open a few routes, too.

What is it that makes a world-famous climbing rendezvous? Fashion, for sure, location, and – most of all – rock. Rocklands' sandstone is stunning, not least because of its colours: vibrant reds, oranges and yellows that combine together beautifully in the strong South African sunlight. But it is also stunning for its optimal shapes, large and rounded with a unique texture that make for a bouldering paradise.

There is not just bouldering to be found here, however. The same rock, at various points across its large expanse, develops into much taller chunks that are crossed by horizontal cracks. These spots make it a perfect destination for the trad climber, too – even more captivating because so much of this area is still to be developed. A few lines have appeared and the first topo book will come out soon, but trad climbing takes more time and dedication – sometimes even years of devotion for one fanatic to crack a line and free it for others to follow. It requires the effort of exploration, trying and cleaning until the line becomes climbable. Sometimes you spend days searching, finding and cleaning a line that appeals to you before realizing that, due to one single movement, it simply cannot work. Sometimes, though, from the moment you lay eyes on a virgin piece of rock and mentally draw a line on the face, everything flows. You find just the right placements to secure yourself, and just enough holds to make it work. You climb it, and from sheer rock something has transformed into a route: your route.

Rocklands' orange rock offers almost endless opportunity for just these moments. Its large expanse and beautiful scenery are a paradise in their own right, but for the climber there is just that little bit more attraction.

Fact File The Cederberg

TYPE OF CLIMB: Bouldering, sport, trad

TYPE OF ROCK: Sandstone

GRADE VARIATION: 5 to 8C;
6a to 8b+; VS to E9

CLIMB LENGTH: Less than 40m

BEST TIME TO CLIMB:
June to August

OTHER NOTABLE CLIMBS:
The Rhino, 7B; Caroline, 7C+; The Tracks,
E7; Bonanno Pisano, E9; The Red Road, E3

1 Rhioferos, E3
2 KaKa-Boom, E6
3 Path de la Giraffe, E6
4 Beware the Beastie, E8
5 Don't Stop Me Now, E1

The Cederberg

FIELDS OF JOY, THE CEDERBERG

FIELDS OF JOY, THE CEDERBERG

FIELDS OF JOY, THE CEDERBERG

RIGHT: James about to start the last hard section on Beware the Beastie, Fields of Joy. A long, but fortunately safe fall awaits should one fail to negotiate the serious of tricky moves on immaculate rock.

Cilaos Réunion Island
Grade variation: 3+ to 8A+; 4+ to 8c+

Limestone, granite, gritstone ... different types of rock are to a climber what different flours are to a baker: a world of possibilities. Limestone is often smooth – almost a varnished finish – whereas if you pass your hand across a gritstone wall, you feel the friction immediately. But basalt is the rock that is most aggressive. Just thinking about the sharp, black rock makes you imagine the abrasions on your skin.

The island of Réunion is a tiny, 100-kilometre-wide dot in the middle of the Indian Ocean. Born from a 'hot spot' in the Earth's mantel, it is one of the lonely volcanoes that have emerged from the oceanic floor, 4,000 metres below the surface of the sea. It is here on this rough, geologically rich ground, exclusively born from basalt, that you realize how close climbing is to nature.

This French island, 12,000 kilometres away from mainland France, is home to people from all around the Indian Ocean. Its natural ravines offer the perfect place to learn to climb, the water helping to smooth over the rock. But it is in the heart of the island, under the village of Cilaos, where the rock changes and offers the biggest challenge. Deep in a gorge sculpted by water made wild during cyclones, you reach the gabbro.

Gabbro is a rock with a similar chemical composition to basalt, but instead of undergoing swift cooling after its eruption, gabbro cools over thousands of years deep underneath the Earth's surface. So while basalt is rough from the instant transformation of magma coming into contact with air and crystallizing it into rock, gabbro by contrast is smooth and dense.

ABOVE: Réunion Island is a land of many faces. From tropical jungle to the crater of a volcano, the scenery and the weather is always changing.

RIGHT: Planning the project before descending into La Chapelle.
FAR RIGHT: Breakfast in basecamp.

ABOVE: James opening a new pitch in Zembrocal. The drill and bolting equipment is left hanging on a bolt below whilst he climbs the next new section.
RIGHT: Abseiling into one of Réunion Island's many ravines.

Fact File Cilaos

TYPE OF CLIMB: Bouldering, sport, multi-pitch

TYPE OF ROCK: Basalt and gabbro

GRADE VARIATION: 3+ to 8A+; 4+ to 8c+

CLIMB LENGTH: 2 to 130m

BEST TIME TO CLIMB: May to August

OTHER NOTABLE CLIMBS:
Legend des Tropiques, 7a

Réunion Island

ZEMBROCAL, LA CHAPELLE, CILAOS

7a

6c

8c+

8a

8a

8a

7a

Below Cilaos, there is a blank rock face at La Chapelle, at the bottom of an intimidating, virgin rocky face, famous on the island for its curious light display from the cascade of water nearby.

'We didn't know it yet, but we would struggle for two weeks to open a route from the bottom of that wall,' says Caroline Ciavaldini. That was the game we had chosen: to create the first route on this virgin, 130-metre wall, starting at the bottom and placing protection as we went. It's a hard method, but it creates the best routes and allows the climber to follow the natural path of the rock. From far away, the rock face looks as if it holds no weaknesses – the numerous cracks appear to allow you passage. Closer in, you realize that the cracks are not cracks at all, just changes of angle that cheat the eye. The compactness of gabbro allows very few holds and very few true cracks. Big, blank faces suddenly jump into a new angle; you can get to the bottom of a section of wall as smooth as glass, and there will be no way to pass. It forces you to go backwards, until you find an evasion line to the left or right. As James Pearson describes, 'The climb was like a jigsaw that we were trying to solve, creating the route as we were going up, using only temporary protection as much as possible.'

After eight tiring days, the team had finally created a vertical path that led them to the top of the cliff. They called their climb Zembrocal. 'From the first day on, we had found only one place to start, in a 200-metre-wide bar, and every evening we would finish the day amazed that we had been able to continue,' recalls Caroline. 'There was only this one line where the weaknesses in the rock were continuous, and it miraculously led us to the top of the crag,' she says.

As teammate Yuji Hirayama remembers, the main challenge was also psychological – the rock almost forced you to give up. 'Any day, we could have finished in a dead end or failed to find a solution and have to give up. But every day, it just about worked. It took us eight more days to succeed in climbing the route cleanly, and that required the tenacity of the whole team.' In the end, Hirayama solved the fifth pitch, the hardest one, in the very last hour of the very last day of the trip.

Opening a route from the bottom is mainly about following the rock, revealing a path that already exists. The basalt and gabbro rocky gorges of Réunion remind you that whether the path will be easy, hard or impossible isn't really down to you and your skill, it's down to nature. Sometimes you get so lucky that you can only say 'thank you'.

LEFT: The ravines of Réunion descend
from the mountain to the sea.
RIGHT: Caroline trying hard on the third
pitch of Zembrocal.

Asia

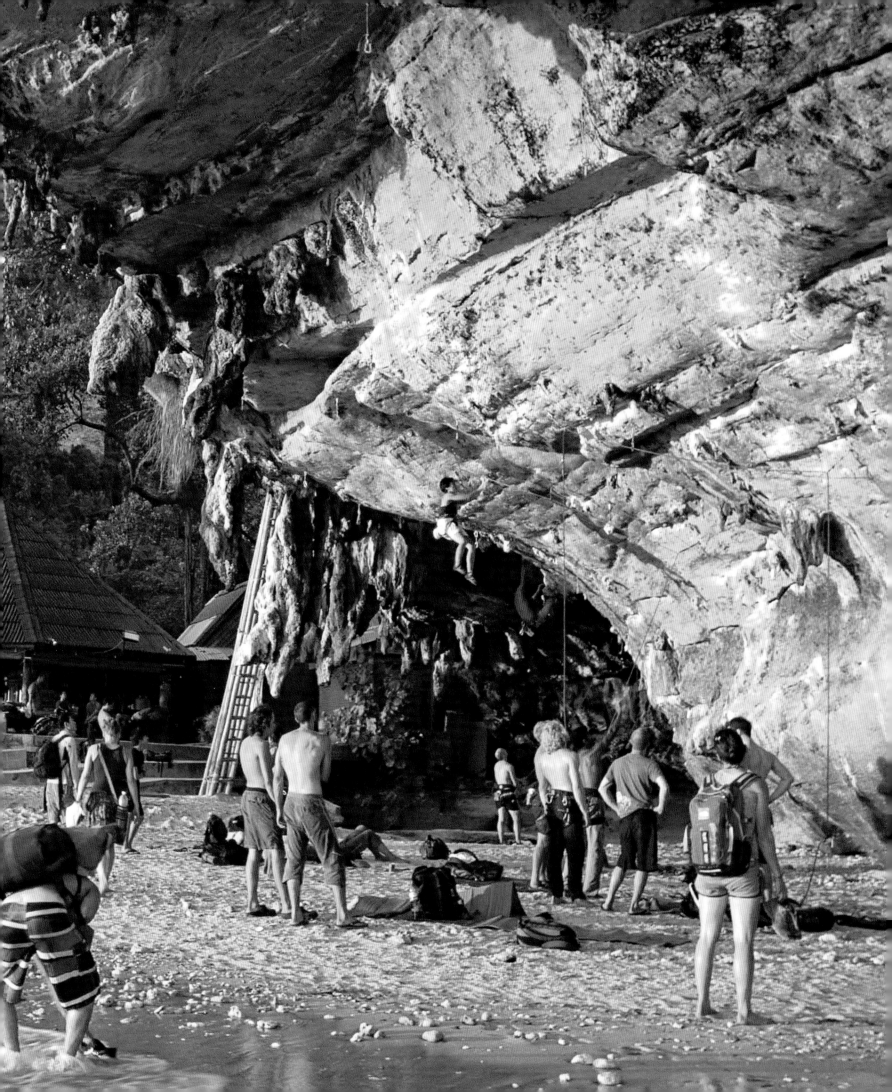

Tonsai Beach Thailand
Grade variation: 4+ to 8c

BELOW: The Railay peninsula is, without doubt, one of the most picturesque places to climb.

Fact File Tonsai Beach

TYPE OF CLIMB: Sport, multi-pitch

TYPE OF ROCK: Limestone

GRADE VARIATION: 4+ to 8c

CLIMB LENGTH: 10 to 100m

BEST TIME TO CLIMB: November to March

OTHER NOTABLE CLIMBS: Jai Dum, 8b; The Groove Tube, 6a; Babes in Thailand, 7a

Tonsai Beach

LORD OF THE THAIS, THAIWAND WALL, TONSAI BEACH

3
6a
7b
7a+
6c+
6a+

As an adventurous climber, it's easy to find yourself envious of the generation before. By the late 1980s, travelling the world had become affordable and there was untouched wonder after untouched wonder just waiting to be discovered. One such place is the Phra Nang peninsula in Thailand. In the early 1990s, Sam Lightner Jr and Todd Skinner visited it and subsequently began the development of Tonsai Beach, which would soon become perhaps the most famous exotic sport-climbing area in the world.

Coming around the headland on your initial approach by longtail boat is a memory that will last a lifetime. The first time you cast your eyes on the picture-perfect scene, you are sure you have come to climbing heaven. Towering, melting limestone walls soar 100 metres out of a turquoise-blue sea, and white, sandy beaches stretch as far as the eye can see. If paradise on Earth exists, this has to be it.

Understandably Tonsai rapidly became the most talked about and visited climbing destination in Southeast Asia. Its incredible success has had many positive implications, but sadly it has also spoilt some of its magic. The once-deserted beach has become overcrowded, the classic routes are more than polished and the local sanitation leaves a lot to be desired.

Many people have written Tonsai off as a sad case of paradise lost, yet for those willing to search a little further, there is still magic and adventure to be found. Whilst sport climbers queue for the classics at Tonsai Roof, amazing and unspoiled multi-pitch routes can be found just a short walk away. The large, yellow face of Thaiwand Wall is located to the east of Tonsai Beach, perched on the gigantic lump of karst between Phra Nang and West Railey. It's home to a bunch of top-quality, powerful, mid-grade routes that climb through amazingly impressive terrain on simply immaculate rock. The multi-pitch routes on Thaiwand Wall are anything but polished, and once you get past the first pitches, which are often climbed as single-pitch routes by sport climbers searching for a bit of peace and quiet, you are almost guaranteed to be on your own.

Of all the routes on Thaiwand Wall, the crown has to go to Lord of the Thais, a fantastic five-pitch 7b that would hold its own with any of the best mid-grade multi-pitches in the world. After three easier first pitches that gradually increase in difficulty, a perfect warm-up for what comes next, you start the crux fourth pitch that has to be seen to be believed.

Not far from the top of the route, a huge, intimidating roof seems to put a halt on all upwards progress. Terrain as impressive as this is usually climbed at a much higher grade, yet as you tentatively reach into the roof, perfect jug after perfect jug present themselves, making the climbing relatively easy, all things considered.

RIGHT: Tom Socias climbing the third pitch of Lord of the Thais.

A travelling climber describes it beautifully: 'Never would I have imagined I could climb something like this,' she said. 'The big overhanging belly looks like something you see climbed by the pros in the movies, not normal people like me. It's intimidating, but it's also Thailand, and so everything seems easy and less stressful. If you fail, so what, so why not try your best? Reaching out and touching the first good hold is a big relief, but not so much as the second, and not so much as the third. Pretty soon you are out there, climbing up this amazing rock and asking yourself how this is possible. That's why we climb, for moments like that. Moments we thought would never happen, and memories that last a lifetime.'

Sitting atop the Thaiwand Wall allows you the chance to 'really' see Tonsai. Whilst the beach and the bars below may be overly crowded, it's the raw beauty of the landscape that makes the Phra Nang peninsula so special. Paradise is still here; it's just a question of changing your perspective.

BELOW: The view from the top.

Ban Nam None Laos
Grade variation: 4+ to 8b

RIGHT: The gentle river passes right by
the bamboo huts at Ban Nam None.

Laos is often overlooked in favour of its better-known neighbours – Thailand, China, Vietnam, even Cambodia – and it is perhaps for that reason that this enchanting, landlocked country has held on to its charms. Long isolated from the rest of the world, its people continue with their relaxed day-to-day lives, and are especially warm and welcoming. Climbing in Laos began close to the cultural capital of Luang Prabang before eventually spreading south, first to Vang Vieng and later down to Thakhek. This surge of development can almost entirely be credited to Volker Schöffl, a German doctor of sports medicine and an avid climber who has spent many years living and working in Laos, and his wife.

During the last ten years, Laos has opened its doors to visiting climbers, and a selection of small 'climbing camps' have popped up around the country. Green Climbers Home is one such place, located close to the small river city of Thakhek. It was opened in 2012 by Tanja and Uli Weidner, a German couple who visited this place during a round-the-world trip, fell in love with it and never left. It is a tranquil little haven, ten kilometres out of town and just 100 metres from the cliffs. A central restaurant is surrounded by several bungalows, and there is even space to put up a few tents. A small shop sells everything you could need – chalk, a topo and basic climbing gear, as well as essential everyday supplies.

With over 100 well-bolted, accessible routes graded from 4+ to 8b, the climbing around Thakhek has enough to please almost everyone. Yet should too many days of the easy life leave you craving something more, adventure is never far away. Motorbikes can be hired from the camp or nearby town, where one can follow 150 kilometres of windy jungle road to Ban Nam None, a tiny village in the middle of nowhere ten kilometres before the famous Kong Lor water cave.

ABOVE: Caroline climbing Onh, 8a.
OPPOSITE: Very few climbers visit here, so the routes can be rather dirty.

Fact File Ban Nam None

TYPE OF CLIMB: Sport

TYPE OF ROCK: Limestone

GRADE VARIATION: 4+ to 8b

CLIMB LENGTH: 12 to 20m

BEST TIME TO CLIMB: November to March

OTHER NOTABLE CLIMBS: LaoLao, 6c; Onh, 8a

Ban Nam None

1 Banane Nonne, 8a

2 Un Singe en Hiver, 7b

2b Sky Pet, 8b

3 Falang en Décomposition, 7c

4 Laobab, 7a

5 Mister Kham, 7b

6 Mr Mouane, 8a

7 Lëë, 7b

8 Du côté de chez Soān, 6b

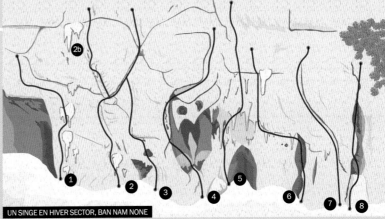

UN SINGE EN HIVER SECTOR, BAN NAM NONE

The climbing in the Ban Nam None valley was developed by a French team in 2006, and many of the routes, especially the harder ones, have still never been free climbed. The rock is a mixture of compact limestone, covered in places by gigantic, dripping tufas. Rarely will a visiting climber have seen them so big. There are tufas on top of tufas on top of tufas, giving the impression that the cliff seems somehow to be melting. The most extreme example of this is the playfully named route Banane Nonne, graded 8a. Starting in a deep, dark, tufa-covered cave, you make your way slowly out towards the light, passing over some of the strangest rock you may ever have touched. Many resting positions can be found by jamming various body parts between the dripping tufas – use them, in order to save a little energy for the final, tough section up to the belay.

Very few people have ever come climbing here so be aware that, due to the lack of traffic, the rock can be very sharp. Vegetation grows fast in the jungle, and animals and insects like to build their homes in the holes. The routes may need a bit of cleaning before you can climb them, and your average toothbrush may not be quite up to the job.

If creating new routes is your thing, there is also plenty of steep, unclimbed rock still to develop – just remember to bring everything with you, as it's impossible to find supplies here. With enough motion, perhaps one day this valley will become a major stopping point on the Southeast Asia climbing circuit. For now, climbing here is an effort, but one that is totally worth it. To be all alone in this world is a rare gift, so make the most of it while you can.

RIGHT: Tufas on top of tufas – the rock of Ban Nam None looks as if it is melting.

Bukit Ketri Malaysia
Grade variation: 6a to 8c+

If you are up for the backpacker's approach to tourism – getting by on snippets of language, a huge backpack and not much money – and add to this a rope, climbing shoes and a specific target, then what you have is the climbing backpacker. If this appeals, then you just might find yourself in the small village of Bukit Ketri in Malaysia, hosted for the night in an open bamboo hut with a simple outdoor tap, a mosquito net and a mat. And you will be a king in this kingdom, welcomed by the village people with warmth.

A row of tables sheltered from the rain form a small *cantina* opposite the mighty crag you are here to climb. The crag is within ten minutes' walk of the main village, but as a climber you will be an unusual attraction for the locals. Bukit Ketri has been bolted by a team of European climbers tipped off by expats in Kuala Lumpur, and they opened all the routes within a few weeks. Since then, however, the rock has mainly been climbed by spiders and monkeys, with just a few visiting climbers occasionally disturbing the cobwebs. Still, one inhabitant fell in love at first sight with the sport, and awaits any occasion to show the routes to new visitors.

Wherever you look in the small state of Perlis you see a plain, broken by high hills. Most of the hills are open in one direction, onto a cave or at least an overhanging wall. Impeccable limestone surrounds you, forming gigantic tufas just begging to be climbed.

RIGHT: Caroline climbing the overhang at Bukit Ketri.

On the hill of Bukit Ketri, however, the cliff is not just covered in tufas but looks more like Swiss cheese, punctuated by holes. It is a strange sight but one that means that there is plenty of access to the cliff and lots of possibilities to test yourself against the crag. The multitude of holes can be reached via natural tunnels and bamboo ladders, the condition of which varies. They were placed many years ago by guano collectors – workers who collected and sold bats' droppings as a pricy fertilizer. Cheaper artificial fertilizers have since halted that line of work, but the ladders remain for the delight (and sometimes fear) of climbers. Some of the routes even include bits of caving through the holes themselves. The crags here are both very unusual and enormous fun.

On the last level, it is possible to reach the harder routes via a dark tunnel that brings you 30 metres up, to the middle of the crag. Be sure to make some noise with a stick to frighten potential snakes.

With this great array of climbs and possibilities the best route is hard to pick, but one certainly stands out. The Belly Button Roof, a 7b+, follows drops of rock within the roof of one of the biggest holes, creating a path that brings you right over the forest. Climbing through terrain that would otherwise be either impossible or extremely hard, this three-dimensional climbing adds to the peculiarity of the route. You finish the route with a lot of air below you and totally disorientated. Turn around and admire the panorama of rice fields, hills and tropical forest below.

The crag is an incredible proposition and proves to be a snapshot of what life is like in Bukit Ketri. This small, relaxed village, miles from the buzz of city life, allows you to climb and explore forever in its holey cliffside.

LEFT: Caroline heading up to the higher levels. The bamboo ladders were originally used by guano collectors, but today help climbers access the various sections of the cliff.
OPPOSITE: Belly Button Roof, the best route of the cliff and one of the best 7b+s in Southeast Asia.

Fact File Bukit Ketri

TYPE OF CLIMB: Sport

TYPE OF ROCK: Limestone

GRADE VARIATION: 6a to 8c+

CLIMB LENGTH: 15 to 30m

BEST TIME TO CLIMB: January to March and June to August

OTHER NOTABLE CLIMBS: There are many virgin crags around to develop

Bukit Ketri

BELLY BUTTON ROOF, BUKIT KETRI

Access via bamboo ladders and cave system

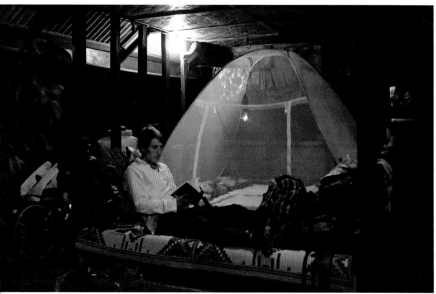

TOP: The adorable family who lives across the street lets visiting climbers put tents up in their backyard.

ABOVE: Home sweet home. It's hot here all year round, so a mosquito net is all you need.

OPPOSITE: James climbing one of the rare giant pillars of Bukit Ketri.

RIGHT: The amazing Donkey Ear. Once home to some of Kinabalu's hardest, most beautiful routes, it fell down during the tragic earthquake of 2015.

Kinabalu Malaysia
Grade variation: 5+ to 9a; VS to E6

ount Kinabalu, Southeast Asia's highest summit with its 4,095
metres of altitude, takes its footing directly off a tropical forest,
next to the coastal city of Kota Kinabalu on the Malaysian side of Borneo.

In a day, you land by the sea, take a couple of hours' bus ride and
then start walking to an approximate altitude of 1,800 metres. Kinabalu
is a popular destination, so the path is well travelled even though it
makes its way through the ever-growing tropical forest. Seven hours
of hiking and over 1,500 metres of vertical gain will bring you to an
altitude hut, where most tourists sleep before the summit push. But as
a climber, your goal isn't just to reach the summit's plain, it's to remain

there and get as much time as possible to explore the endless amounts
of granite. Above 3,000 metres you have reached the limit of vegetation,
and here only lichens survive the altitude and its harsh conditions. The
plateau that caps Kinabalu is a mineral universe, with granite plains,
spikes, domes, towers and canyons.

A last, tiny hut right beneath two donkey's ears – proud towers
that dominate the sloping ground – offers shelter and relative
warmth. Bunk beds, a simple kitchen and outside toilets are
all the comfort a climber can get after a cold, windy day
on the desolate plateau. Here, the sun can be obscured

in minutes by the mist running up the gullies that flank the sides of the plateau. It is mist so dense that you can't see ten metres ahead, in which case you can follow a white tread that runs back to the hut, craving a hot cup of tea.

Kinabalu is a world of silence and patience. To climb there, you have to accept that it will be cold, and jump on every appearance of the sun to attempt your route. One climber in particular has had the patience to come here year after year, and he has put Kinabalu firmly on the climber's map.

Yuji Hirayama is a 47-year-old Japanese climber, and his endless list of achievements has made him a hero and a legend in the climbing world. From world championships and speed records to Yosemite firsts and the first 8c on-sight in history, Hirayama has mastered most aspects of the very diverse sport that is climbing. He approaches it with a powerful mix of calmness, spirituality, detachment and focus.

Yuji has returned to Kinabalu four times so far, opening and succeeding on Pogulian Do Koduduo, the first 9a of Southeast Asia. He even chased after his dream of the next grade there with Tinipi, a route that he opened and offered to Daniel Woods. Tinipi, realized and graded by Woods at 9a+, was Yuji's dream route, a marvellous, intense proposition on one of the donkey's ears that sadly fell apart during the devastating earthquake of 2015.

Yuji wants to go back anyway, largely for the granite that is so pure it is almost perfect, cleansed by the water and winds that regularly storm through the plateau and take with them any imperfection. He also returns, of course, for the people, the guides and the guardians of Kinabalu.

TOP RIGHT: The thick, white rope leading all the way to the summit. An eyesore, or a lifeline for tourists lost in the mist?

RIGHT: Caroline making her way back to the Pendan Hut, our home for three weeks during our visit in 2012.

LEFT: Daniel Woods warming up on the classic Little Pretty.

LEFT: Yuji Hirayama taking a big fall off Pogulian Do Koduduo.

ABOVE: The summit plateau of Mount Kinabalu.

Fact File Kinabalu

TYPE OF CLIMB: Sport routes, multi-pitch, trad

TYPE OF ROCK: Perfect granite

GRADE VARIATION: 5+ to 9a; VS to E6

CLIMB LENGTH: 10 to 150m

BEST TIME TO CLIMB: May to June offers the most stable weather, but it is possible to climb all year round

OTHER NOTABLE CLIMBS: Ginza, E2; Metisse, E6; Excalibur, 8c+

Kinabalu

POGULIAN DO KODUDUO, MOUNT KINABALU

9a

7c+

El Nido Palawan, Philippines
Grade variation: 6b to 8a

Certain climbing trips are all about performance, focus and hard climbing. A route at your very limit will demand that you dig deep and search for solutions that test you. They are challenging and demand your full skill set. Other trips might take you to an unknown country, where grades don't matter or simply don't exist. These trips are the ones that bring you back to climbing for the sheer joy of it, where you can appreciate the beauty of efficient movement and the simple pleasure of being in the moment.

With the South China Sea crashing against its sides, the beautiful Philippine island of Palawan not only has stunning beaches, but also a limestone so incredible that it is hard to believe it has been so rarely climbed.

The town of El Nido, at the northernmost tip of Palawan, is famous for its perfect sand and tropical coral reef. It is a place where electricity only runs in the mornings due to power shortages, and traditional biscuits from the bakery provide the last sustenance available before embarking for the dots of islands that are reached via bamboo motorized boat or, for those so inclined, a kayak. On this turquoise sea, the water is so clear that you can check the depth without a mask. There are an incredible forty-five islands and islets here, the coasts of which are either beaches or limestone cliffs. The limestone often overhangs, forming huge caves and dripping tufas. It is all there, waiting to be revealed.

The cliffs need studying first – analyzing to see if there are enough holds to begin climbing. On every first ascent, it's entirely up to you

– and the rock – to decide the path that the route will take. You can putter on your boat around every island, searching for the piece of rock that most appeals. The 'white wall' on Lagen Island displays a single column running 20 metres straight up from the sea. It is steep, but the column is just good enough to make the climbing achievable, albeit still precarious. The rock is brand new – washed by the waves. It's essential that you pick your spot well, with deep-enough water beneath. Breaking holds on this type of rock is common, meaning that unexpected falls are frequent and a confident water landing is essential.

This is deep-water soloing, a spicy style of climbing. There is no rope, just your climbing shoes and the water to catch you if you fall. It takes a good climber around ten minutes to reach the top of the tufa, and it's an emotional climb, requiring full concentration and more than a few dynamic movements. But it is an exhilarating experience to be at that height with only you, the rock and the wind for company. Reaching the top of the climb there is a small ledge, which requires nerves of steel once more – your downward route is a 'simple' jump back into the water a good 20 metres below you. To land smoothly, prepare to enter the water very straight, with legs together, arms crossed, relaxed and certainly not looking down. This is essential to avoid injury at that height, and a skill to be learned with great caution.

After such a free climb, that piece of rock becomes transformed in your mind from mere rock into a route where you lived an adventure. You leave no trace bar a bit of chalk that the sea wind will soon erase, and maybe a photograph, a line drawn on it to remember the route. A grade? In this part of the world and with this sort of climbing, it seems neither necessary nor appropriate. The next climber will choose his own holds, perhaps a different height to stop at. That is the exhilaration of climbing in El Nido, a virgin deep-water-soloing playground. And perhaps that is the essence of this particular discipline: giving back to a climber their own choice of the route, the line, the holds and the challenge.

LEFT: James trying a line that attracted his eye on Lagen Island, El Nido. When there are so many possibilities, the hardest decision is choosing your line.

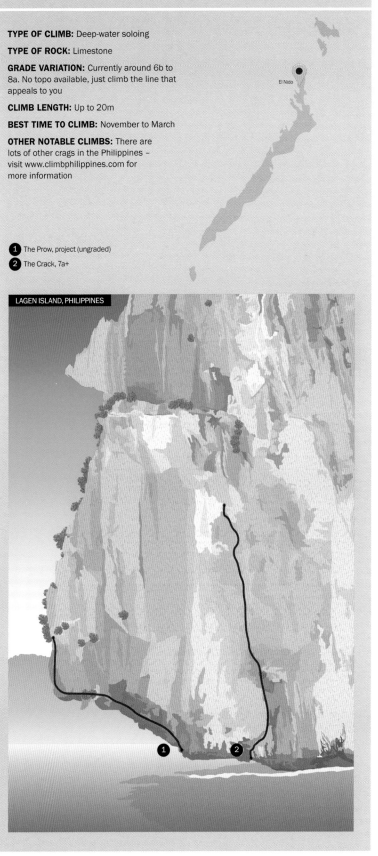

Fact File El Nido

TYPE OF CLIMB: Deep-water soloing

TYPE OF ROCK: Limestone

GRADE VARIATION: Currently around 6b to 8a. No topo available, just climb the line that appeals to you

CLIMB LENGTH: Up to 20m

BEST TIME TO CLIMB: November to March

OTHER NOTABLE CLIMBS: There are lots of other crags in the Philippines – visit www.climbphilippines.com for more information

El Nido

1 The Prow, project (ungraded)
2 The Crack, 7a+

LAGEN ISLAND, PHILIPPINES

Kinkasan Miyagi, Japan
Grade variation: VS to E7

Kinkasan cannot be found on any climbing map. Few climbers have ever visited this magical place, and even fewer routes have been established, yet the potential for development and the purity of the rock make Kinkasan a glimmering jewel in the eyes of adventurous climbers the world over.

RIGHT: Caroline working a project on the sea cliffs of Kinkasan.

Fact File Kinkasan

TYPE OF CLIMB: Trad or bouldering

TYPE OF ROCK: Granite sea cliffs

GRADE VARIATION: VS to E7 – most of it is still to be developed

CLIMB LENGTH: Less than 50m

BEST TIME TO CLIMB: October to November

OTHER NOTABLE CLIMBS: Light, E7; Rainy With a Chance of Leeches, E6

Kinkasan

1 Well Dunne Dave, HVS
2 The Fallen Phantom, E6

EAST COAST, KINKASAN

Kinkasan, a tiny island in the Miyagi prefecture in northeastern Japan, is considered one of the three holiest places of the Tōhoku region. Home to the 1,300-year-old Koganeyamajinja shrine, and said to bring wealth and riches to all those who visit for three consecutive years, Kinkasan is also commonly called Takarajima – Japanese for Treasure Island.

Kinkasan was once tended by 20 Shinto monks, who held daily prayer ceremonies in its shrine and provided spiritual guidance to the island's multitude of visitors, sometimes as many as 3,000 per day. To cater for so many guests, an abundance of small hotels and restaurants used to be found along the shoreline, and with basic roads running around the entire perimeter, Kinkasan enjoyed a healthy, self-sustaining economy.

However, in March 2011, tensions accumulated at the limit of the Pacific plate and the Continental plate suddenly released, causing an earthquake so powerful that it moved the island of Japan itself. The 8.9-magnitude earthquake caused the ocean floor to rise by ten metres over an area the size of Yorkshire. The displacement of the ocean created giant waves, some crashing into land up to 40 metres above the usual sea level and travelling over ten kilometres inland, devastating everything in their path.

The island of Kinkasan was one of the closest to the epicentre, and as a result its coast was almost totally destroyed. Any infrastructure close to the water's edge was washed away without trace, and due to the destabilization of the land, many of the buildings that escaped the initial shock later crumbled and fell into the sea. Efforts are under way to rebuild and reconstruct, but progress is painfully slow. Visitors to Kinkasan have fallen to just five per cent of their previous number, and there are now only two monks living permanently at the shrine.

Shinto is the ethnic religion of the people of Japan, and is an action-centred religion, focused on ritual practices that establish a connection between present-day Japan and its ancient past. Shinto focuses on the connection between oneself and whatever task one may be doing, trying to find perfection in even the smallest detail. With such a mammoth task ahead of them, one could easily forgive the monks and the small community of volunteers on Kinkasan for giving up hope and moving

OPPOSITE: Caroline making the first ascent of our first new route. Unclimbed granite is often dirty, but here the rock was perfect.

ABOVE: One of the abandoned hotels on Kinkasan.

away, yet the reality of their actions is the exact opposite. Slowly but surely, things are moving forward. Everyone plays their part, does their best and gives whatever help they can.

In 2015, professional Japanese climber Yuji Hirayama visited the island after being contacted by a local non-profit organization called First Ascent Japan. They hoped that the untouched sea cliffs of Kinkasan had the potential to produce fantastic traditional climbing routes, and wanted Yuji to develop and promote climbing on the island with the eventual goal of providing a new source of adventure tourism. Impressed by both the quality and quantity of the rock, as well as the wild, unspoiled nature of the island, Yuji vowed to return the following year with a bigger team to continue the development – doing his part in the best way he could.

Just like the reconstruction effort, climbing on Kinkasan is developing slowly but surely. With unclimbed sea cliffs of perfect white granite, split by regular clean cracks and stretching as far as the eye can see, Kinkasan offers an almost unlimited potential for new routes. With its complicated access, costly accommodation and long approach hikes, climbing on Kinkasan demands a little more effort than the average destination. Yet for those willing to go the extra mile, the rewards are huge. For climbers, at least, Kinkasan really is a treasure island.

BELOW: Hiking back through the fairytale forest after a long, wet day exploring.

RIGHT: Caroline peeping through a splitter crack.

Australasia

The Grampians Victoria, Australia
Grade variation: 3+ to 8C; 14 to 34

Australia is big. Really, really big. And although Australia can boast some of the best rock on the planet, it's one of the climbing world's least-visited areas. There is a lot of incredible climbing to be found Down Under, especially for climbers who enjoy a little adventure, but the low density of areas across the country, as well as the general distance away from anywhere else in the world, make it hard for many travelling climbers to reach it.

In the world of climbing this rarity is something to be savoured. With many thousands of incredible routes, in all styles and on all types of rock, yet with very few climbers, Australia can be climbing heaven for those in search of a relaxing atmosphere and almost unlimited potential.

The majority of Australian climbing is situated in the southeastern coastal region, between the thriving metropolises of Melbourne and Sydney. Yet despite mirroring almost perfectly the distribution of the general Australian population, the crags are rarely busy thanks to climbing being quite low on the Australian sporting community's radar. You could be fighting for space on a congested Sydney beach or crammed into an overcrowded stadium to watch cricket or Aussie rules football, but climbers need only drive a few miles up into the hills to have the place to themselves.

The most famous and iconic of Australian climbing venues is undoubtedly the Grampians National Park. Situated 300 kilometres west of Melbourne, the Grampians offer more climbs in one general location than any other area in the country, and enjoy a quality of rock that many have muttered to be the best in the world. A bullet-hard, fine-grained red sandstone, it sometimes seems to have more in common with perfect, water-sculpted limestone. It is the stuff of which climbers' dreams are made, and is a real pleasure to climb on. It's a rock that forms amazing holds and lines and just eats up traditional protection.

LEFT: James making the mandatory dyno on Mirage (27) on the Taipan Wall.

RIGHT: Passport to Insanity is one of Australia's most iconic routes, and can be found right in the heart of the Grampians.

As one might expect from an Australian national park, the Grampians is rather large and so a car really is a must if you plan to explore even a small part of its potential. However, with so much space comes both seclusion and diversity. Here it is possible not only to climb in almost every style imaginable, from bouldering to sport to trad, but also to do it completely alone. Hiking around the Grampians is a pleasure in itself, with an abundance of incredible wildlife and other amazing sights. After a hard day's cragging, the climber will be able to cool off with a swim under one of the park's many picturesque waterfalls – don't worry, you'd struggle to find a crocodile here. In common with other areas of Australian bush, however, it is home to many poisonous snakes and spiders, which can be quite common during the hotter summer months. The poisonous snakes especially are no joke: the Grampians are home to both red-bellied black and eastern brown snakes, which are extremely venomous – so be careful.

With so many routes to choose from, it's hard to pick out one to recommend over another. However, the routes on Taipan Wall offer especially rewarding climbs. Its main route, the classic 8a Serpentine, is a route that should be on any upper-grade sport-climber's dream list, and Mirage is an amazing trad route with a huge, two-metre dyno. With a whole host of five-star routes in all different styles, Taipan Wall has to be a contender for one of the best cliffs in the world.

Slightly further off the beaten track lies Eureka Wall, home to some of the best low- to mid-grade trad routes around. Like Taipan Wall, almost every route here is good, yet Archimedes' Principle – a pure trad route that draws a striking line up the middle of a very unlikely looking blank face – has to be climbed to be believed. Simply amazing.

LEFT: Rock doesn't get much better than this. Matt Segal ascending the famous Red Sail in the Grampians.
NEXT PAGE: James climbing one of the best routes on the planet – Archimedes' Principle on the Eureka Wall.

Fact File The Grampians

TYPE OF CLIMB: Bouldering, sport, trad

TYPE OF ROCK: Quartzite

GRADE VARIATION: 3+ to 8C; 14 to 34

CLIMB LENGTH: 2 to 40m

BEST TIME TO CLIMB: April to September

OTHER NOTABLE CLIMBS:
Serpentine, 8a

Grampians National Park

ARCHIMEDES' PRINCIPLE, EUREKA WALL, THE GRAMPIANS

23

25

20

The Totem Pole
Cape Huay, Tasmania

Grade variation: 24 to 30

BELOW: The stunning scenery of Tasmania and the Cape Pillar, looking down to the Trident and across to Tasman Island.

Fact File The Totem Pole

TYPE OF CLIMB: Adventure, multi-pitch

TYPE OF ROCK: Dolerite

GRADE VARIATION: 24 to 30

CLIMB LENGTH: 60m

BEST TIME TO CLIMB: April to September

OTHER NOTABLE CLIMBS:
The Ewbank Route, 30;
The Free Route, 25

Cape Huay

DEEP PLAY, THE TOTEM POLE

Set up Tyrolean traverse here with abseil rope

Abseil to base and swing across; keep abseil rope clipped to harness

There are few pieces of rock around the world as iconic as the Totem Pole. The towering walls of Yosemite National Park may beat it for sheer scale and the many towers of Metéora, with their monasteries on top, may steal the crown for pure, mysterious beauty. Nowhere, though, can touch the Totem Pole for its simple, mind-bogglingly strange placement and oddly tall, thin structure.

Situated off the southeastern coast of Tasmania, the Totem Pole is one of the last pieces of solid land before the vast Southern Ocean and the frozen nothingness of Antarctica. This raw and exposed position leaves the Totem Pole at the mercy of some of the worst weather that Mother Nature can muster, and it is precisely this extreme weather that has created this curious pile of stones in the first place.

Detached from the mainland by approximately three metres at the base and 15 metres at the top, the Totem Pole rises over 60 metres directly out of the churning ocean, and is never more than four metres wide. For adventurous climbers around the world, the Totem Pole is right at the top of the 'dream list', and almost every climber who makes the long and arduous journey to it agrees that the effort involved was more than worth it.

To access the Totem Pole, one must first drive to a remote parking area in Fortescue Bay, then hike for two hours along a well-cut jungle track towards Cape Huay. On reaching this remote spot, a bolted belay point will be found on the cliff top, opposite the tower, from where you can assess the condition of the sea before rappelling down to begin the climb.

At this point in the adventure it can be tempting to throw caution to the wind, but serious respect must be given to the power of the sea.

Even in calm conditions, a rogue wave capable of soaking the belayer is a common occurrence. In bad weather, the waves can be so big that they reach the top of the first pitch, with the spray going higher than the tower itself. Consider this a stern warning!

Once at the base of the tower, and using the fixed abseil rope, you must swing out across the void to grab a couple of conveniently placed bolts. Thanking whoever so considerately placed these metal rings many years ago, cross your fingers that the sea remains calm, arrange your climbing gear as quickly as possible, and whatever you do, don't let go of the abseil rope.

The first pitch of Deep Play, the easiest route on the Totem Pole, is a precarious, off-balance finger crack that feels a lot tougher than the suggested grade of 24. At around 25 metres, the sanctuary of a large, flat belay ledge offers an opportunity to breathe, and at the same time realize just exactly how much of a crazy position you have got yourself into. As Sonnie Trotter said in 2016, 'When you get on it you're kind of vulnerable, because there's nowhere to go. There's nothing you can do at that point. Once you're on "the Tote" there's nowhere to hide.'

Once enough courage has been found, the second pitch – which includes over 40 metres of some of the best climbing known to man – will take the successful climber towards the top of the tower. Perhaps it is the absurdity of the situation that makes you more receptive to the pleasure, but it really is five-star climbing. Continuously interesting moves on beautiful, smooth, sculpted holds; it is the stuff that climbers dream of. On reaching the summit of the tower, you have the feeling that you are an astronaut out in space, looking back to Earth. Such a strange place – detached, inhospitable but unimaginably, undeniably beautiful.

After soaking up everything you can from your trip to outer space, it's time to drop out of orbit and begin the exciting, heart-in-mouth journey back to Earth. After scrambling back down to the last of the bolted belays, just below the summit of the tower, you can set up a sort of circus tightrope that climbers call a Tyrolean traverse to take you back to the mainland. After one last check that all is in order, clip your harness into the line, jump out into the abyss and pull yourself back to solid ground and glory.

Glossary

abseil: also called a **rappel** after its French name. A controlled descent of a vertical drop, such as a rock face, using a rope and abseil device. Climbers use this technique when it is the only way down after (or before – in Verdon, for example) a route. It is also the way bolters access the rock when bolting, unless they decided to bolt from the ground up.

aid climbing: a style of climbing in which standing on or pulling oneself up via devices attached to fixed or temporary protection is used. The term contrasts with free climbing, in which progress is made without using any artificial aids.

blobs: small, round rock concretions usually formed in limestone caves, as the calcite recrystallizes after having been dissolved in the passing water.

bloc: an alternate word for **boulder**.

bolt: a permanent anchor fixed into a hole drilled in the rock. The climber clips a **quickdraw** into it, and then their rope into the quickdraw. Most bolts are either expansion bolts or glued in place with liquid resin. The bolter will create a route by bolting.

boulder: a boulder, as opposed to a route, is a short rock face (less than eight metres) climbed without a harness or rope. The climber will usually be protected by crash pads.

bouldering mat (or crash pad): a foam pad placed at the foot of a boulder when bouldering. In the event of a fall, the climber aims to land on the mat to avoid injury, aided by their **spotter**. There are various sizes and makes, but the most common type is a folded mattress, 8–10 centimetres thick, that when unfolded measures about 1 by 1.3 metres. Most bouldering mats have shoulder straps, so as to move it easily between boulders.

chipping: a technique that uses a hammer and chisel (or a drill) to create artificial holds on natural rock. This is extremely controversial within the climbing community because it permanently modifies the natural features of a rock face. In the past the practice was accepted or ignored, as there seemed to be an infinite amount of rock available and indoor climbing gyms didn't exist. But as the sport grows and environmental concerns become more prominent, there has been a trend against chipping. This process can also be referred to as 'manufacturing' holds.

crimp: a very small, in-cut finger hold where the climber has to arch (crimp) his fingers.

crux: the most difficult or challenging section of a route. A route may comprise several cruxes. There are also routes, however, that have a very consistent level of difficulty with no sections that stand out as harder than the rest.

deep-water soloing (DWS) (or psicobloc): a form of solo rock climbing that has water (lake or sea) at the base of the route. Were the climber to fall, they would land in the water. The water must therefore be of sufficient depth, and the climber can't go much higher than 25 metres, above which height falling into the water is very dangerous.

dyno: a dynamic movement in which one's body is detached from the rock. Could also be called a jump.

free climbing: an ascent that involves holding onto and stepping on only natural features of the rock (the holds), using rope and equipment only to catch the climber in case of a fall, via a belayer. **Sport climbing** and **trad climbing** are both free climbing.

free-solo: *see* **soloing**

ground up: an ethical approach to climbing a route, a boulder or a multi-pitch. It means that the climber will not allow himself to inspect any hold with a rope placed above him before trying the route.

hooks (or skyhooks): little metal hooks that the climber will place carefully on a protrusion, before putting his weight on the hook. Usually this device is used in **aid climbing**, but also during ground-up route opening, when the climber will rest on the hook while drilling a hole for a bolt.

huecos: strange, round-shaped 'holes' that often form good holds. Refers to the formations in Hueco Tanks State Park.

jug: a very good hold.

karst: a landscape formed from the dissolution of soluble rocks. It is characterized by underground drainage systems with sinkholes and caves, but what climbers search for are the rock towers that are also formed in the process.

lead: a lead climber attaches himself to a dynamic (elastic) climbing rope and ascends a route while periodically placing protection (**quickdraws** or traditional protection) to the rock and clipping his rope into it. The lead climber must have another person acting as a belayer, who will hold the rope in case of a fall.

multi-pitch: a long climb with more than one

pitch. The climber climbs the first pitch and is then joined by their partner, from where they keep on going up via pitch two, three, four and so on.

off-width: a crack too wide to 'jam' and too narrow to 'chimney'. It involves jamming with an entire leg, an arm or a combination of body parts.

portaledge: a portable 'ledge' that a climber can haul with them and use to sleep on during multi-day, multi-pitch climbs.

pro (or protection): safety equipment used by climbers. It can refer to such items as nylon webbing, metal nuts, cams, bolts, pitons, etc.

psicobloc: see **deep-water soloing**

quickdraw: a piece of kit made of two carabiners linked via a sling. It is used to allow the climbing rope to run freely through bolt anchors or other protection while leading. The straight-gate carabiner is clipped to the protection; a bent gate is used for the rope.

rack (or trad rack): collection of traditional climbing protection that the climber will bring up on their harness when climbing. Normally the climber pre-selects the pieces that seem the most appropriate for their route, and doesn't bring every protection available in his bag.

rappel: see **abseil**

refugio (or refuge): mountain accommodation, often inaccessible by road.

run out: a lengthy distance between two points of protection (while leading) which in

some, but not all, cases might be perceived as frightening or dangerous. May also be used as an adjective to describe a route, or a section of a route.

sandbagging: the act of purposefully under-grading a climb.

slab climbing: a type of rock climbing where the rock is at an angle less steep than vertical. It is characterized by balance- and friction-dependent moves on very small holds. Footholds are the most important.

sloper: a (usually) large, flat hold where friction between the rock and the skin of your hand is very important.

smear: a foothold with no obvious feature. Friction between the rubber of your climbing shoe and the rock is very important.

soloing: a style of climbing in which the climber climbs alone, without somebody belaying them. A fall would therefore not be protected, and most likely be lethal.

sport climbing: climbing protected by in-situ, permanent bolts in the rock, plus ropes and quickdraws. The most common style of climbing.

spotting: a safety technique for bouldering. The spotter stands below the climber, with arms raised or at the ready. If the climber falls, the spotter does not catch the climber, but redirects the climber's fall so that they land safely on the bouldering mat.

topo (or topographic): refers to the graphical representation (sketch drawing or a photograph with routes depicted) of a climbing route. It

informs the climber of the grades, directions, lengths and any specifics (such as protection). It is also used for a climbing guidebook of a crag or climbing area in which most routes are described graphically by such topos.

traditional (or trad) climbing: a style of rock climbing in which a climber places, while climbing, all the gear required to protect himself in case of a fall, and removes it when he has finished climbing. Trad climbing requires specific temporary protection such as friends or nuts.

Index

Acknowledgements

W hen Aurum approached us to write a book based on our climbing adventures, everything seemed to fall into place. We'd been hesitating to undertake a project like this for several years, as although we had the stories and the photos, we lacked the necessary publishing knowledge and the courage to jump right in. Aurum brought with them over 40 years of experience in the publishing world, and have been with us every step of the way. We'd like to thank them here, especially Lucy Warburton and Vanessa Green, of The Urban Ant, for helping to make one of our dreams come true.

Special thanks go to our friends who helped us out with some of the chapters – Tom Randal for the White Rim; Arnaud Petit for Salto Angel; Iker and Eneko Pou for Montserrat; Jakopo Larcher for the Rätikon; Ondra Beneš for the Elbe Valley; and Gaz Parry for Prohodna Cave.

We would also like to thank all the other people who made this book possible: our parents for passing on their love of nature and their spirit for exploration; our friends for being with us on the many adventures – may there be many more in the future!; the many photographers who have shared their amazing work and given us thousands of memories to last a lifetime; and finally our sponsors for supporting us through the years, as without them most of these stories would never have happened.

James Pearson and Caroline Ciavaldini

Picture Credits

Every effort has been made to contact copyright holders. However, the publishers will be glad to rectify in future editions any inadvertent omissions brought to their attention.

© 300bolts/manu prats: 92 (top), 93, 94–5, 96–7, 98, 99
© Zorbey Aktuyun: 151
© Keith Bradbury: 127
© Andrew Burr: 24, 25, 28, 29
© Jordi Canyigueral: 100–1, 102, 103, 104–5
© Jimmy Chin: 154–5, 156–7
© Di Dawson (Wikimedia Commons): 38 (bottom)
© Richard Felderer: 8–9, 59, 60–1, 62, 63, 111, 112, 113, 114–5, 116–7, 120, 128, 130, 164, 165, 166–7, 168–9 (top), 169 (bottom left), 170, 171, 172, 173
© FotoVertical: 70, 71, 72–3, 144–5, 146, 148–9, 200
© Raphaël Fourau: 80–1, 82–3, 84, 85
© Jakub Fric: 132–3, 134, 135, 136–7
© Eddie Gianelloni: 30, 31, 32, 33, 64–5, 202–3, 204, 205, 206, 207
© Neil Hart: 86, 87, 88
© Mike Hutton Photography: 26–7
© Nicolas Kalisz: 47 (top)
© Tim Kemple/timkemple.com: Front cover, 2–3, 6–7, 12–13, 15 (bottom right), 16–17, 18–19, 21, 22–3, 34–5, 36–7, 106–7, 108–9, 208–9, 210, 211, 212–3, 214–5
© Jacapo Larcher: 118–9, 122–3
© Damiano Levati/The North Face: 169 (bottom right)
© Talo Martin/Muerdago Films: 90–1, 92 (bottom)
© Ben Moon: 125
© Once Upon A Climb: Back cover, 1, 10, 14, 15 (left; top right), 48–9, 152–3, 158–9, 160–1, 162, 163, 174–5, 176–7, 178–9, 180–1, 182–3, 184, 185, 186–7, 188–9, 190, 191, 192, 193, 194–5, 196, 197, 198, 199, 216–7, 218, 219
© Christian Peters/Shutterstock.com: 40
© Arnaud Petit: 42–3, 45, 47 (bottom)
© Simon Richardson: 126
© David Simmonite: 51, 52–3, 54, 55, 56–7, 66–7, 68, 69, 129
© Ruslan Vakrilov: 139, 140–1, 142, 143
© Evrard Wendenbaum: 46
© Wikimedia Commons: 38 (top)
© www.darksky-media.com: 74–5, 76–7, 78, 79
Page 11: Grade table based on material provided by Rockfax
Page 139: Map route based on material provided at www.climbingguidebg.com and by Nikolay Petkov